HUMAN TECHNOLOGY

Books by Ilchi Lee

Healing Society
Twelve Enlightenments for Healing Society
Brain Respiration
Peaceology
Songs of Enlightenment
Mago's Dream
Healing Chakra
Meridian Exercise for Self-Healing Book 1
Meridian Exercise for Self-Healing Book 2
Dahnhak Kigong
Wisdom of the Chun Bu Kyung

HUMAN TECHNOLOGY

A TOOLKIT FOR
AUTHENTIC LIVING

ILCHI LEE

Healing Society

Healing Society

60 Piki Drive
Sedona, Arizona, 86336
www.hspub.com

First hardcover edition June 2005
Library of Congress Control Number: 2005926514
ISBN: 1-932843-11-6

First trade paperback edition June 2005
Library of Congress Control Number: 2005927706
ISBN: 1-932843-12-4

Manufactured in the United States of America

If you are unable to order this book from your local book seller,
You may order directly from the publisher at 928-204-1106 or
www.hspub.com.

Acknowledgements

My deepest appreciation to my friends and students
who have walked the road of peace
with me for the past twenty-five years.
You have been the source of my inspiration.
To Neale Donald Walsch who advised
me throughout the making of this book.
I thank you for your generous support.
And to my family—my parents, my wife, and two sons—
who have been my greatest supporters.
I wish to express my gratitude and love.

Contents

Foreword

The greatest tool we have for healing our lives is ourselves.

This is something that is widely known, but not widely understood. Knowledge is one thing, understanding is something else altogether. We can know many things, but if we do not understand what we know, all of our knowledge will be for naught. It will have very limited application.

Wisdom is knowledge *applied*.

This book explores some very practical ways in which our knowledge about human beings may be applied. It is entirely possible that the application of this knowledge can produce a better life for all of us—a life without undo dependency on exterior systems or aids, interventions, or pills.

The assertion of this text is that every human being is created to be totally self-sufficient, self-healing, and self-sustaining—and completely capable of total self-realization in a single lifetime. What stops many people from experiencing this extraordinary truth is lack of specific skills and techniques in using the fundamental mechanisms of life and of the body to perform the basic tasks of mental and physical health maintenance.

Part of the problem has been that we have put so much focus in our world on curing the ills of our society that we have all but ignored the most effective path to dealing with those ills: prevention.

Humanity's well-being depends on humanity being well, and a startling percentage of human beings are not. It could be argued (and it has been) that this is because of the high cost of medical treatments and care, which most of the world's people cannot afford. Yet these treatments and this care are nearly always in *response* to ill health, rather than in *prevention* of it. Prevention, it turns out, costs very little.

What has been needed is some sort of codification of prevention techniques that the average person could access, understand, and apply. What has been missing is easily obtainable and reliable information on a *system* of health maintenance that anyone could utilize. In short, what we've required are the *tools* with which to construct a healthful reality.

Now let us be clear about something very important here. The finding of these tools, and the use of them, is more than a matter of individual importance. The entire conglomerate known as *humanity* is at a crossroads regarding its collective well-being. The mental and physical health of our *species as a whole* is now at stake. That is what I meant when I said that humanity's well-being depends on humanity being well.

We are not well now, that is clear. We are behaving with each other in ways that reflect a profound *lack* of well-being. People who are living peacefully in health, harmony, and happiness do not treat each other as we humans currently do. Our society is degenerating around us. We see this slow but sure disintegration and do not know what to do about it. There is a wound in the body human, and it is all we can do to find a band-aid, much less prevent further injury.

This book is about preventing further injury. It is about placing us back on the road to individual good health and collective well-being.

Not every single word or technique found here may be suitable in equal measure to every single person. Indeed, some of the approaches described here are tools that I (and many people in the Western world) have never even heard of. I, therefore, cannot personally endorse or vouch for them. Put simply, *I don't know* whether they work or not. But am I intrigued by the possibilities they offer? You bet. Am I grateful for the opportunities for discovery that they present? Yes, indeed.

We have much to remember of our basic and instinctual awareness of what it is to be fully and functionally human, and I am grateful to Dr. Ilchi Lee for stepping into this void and providing us with a menu of possibilities many of us have never explored.

Neale Donald Walsch

Author's Note

"Great light is invisible, great sound is inaudible."

A light that is too bright cannot be seen, and a sound that is too loud cannot be heard. Truth is always self-evident. However, because of its very obviousness, often we do not acknowledge it. Instead, we continue to live the illusions created by preconceptions and biases, simply out of habit.

In order to create a better life, we must challenge ourselves with hard questions about our lives. Is the way we are currently living the best way there is? Is it a life that is genuinely natural and humane? Is our life authentic, or is it unexamined?

We have created ever more complex systems in the name of comfort and security. Insidiously, we begin trying to match our lives to systems. The most important questions of your life are too precious to be answered by anyone but you. Ideally, institutions and specialists should exist to assist in the *self-education* of the individual. Each individual must recover her sense of mastery over her own life. Only then will technology serve humanity instead of reigning over us.

In this volume, I present a toolkit of Human Technology skills to help you gain confidence in managing the core issues of your life: health, sexuality, and life purpose. They are a starting point, not the final answer. My sincerest wish is that Human Technology aid in the recovery of education, relationships, and harmony between humanity and nature.

We carry a deep wish to create a healthier, happier, and more peaceful society. I believe in the power of this wish. I believe that the people who nurture this wish by the choices and actions that stem from their courageous insights make history.

The most valuable legacy that we can pass on to future generations is the recovery of our humanity so that they can experience a deeper and more meaningful existence. With the power of the Human Technology skills outlined in this book, we can make this legacy a reality in our lifetime.

Ilchi Lee

HUMAN TECHNOLOGY

1

Why Human Technology

TODAY'S WORLD HAS MANY MESSENGERS seeking to tell people about life and how to make it better. Some of these are political, spiritual, or educational figures bringing messages of improved ways to conduct business, education, or deal with our environment. Yet, despite the global impact of these teachers and their respective movements, even with all the individual awakenings, there has only been a slight shift in the global human consciousness.

Of course, this is better than no progress at all, and I pay tribute to the various leaders who have dedicated their lives to and created initiatives for the purpose of bettering this world. I, too, have endeavored as a teacher, and in spite of the more than twenty years of labor, my sense of urgency has never abated. I am distraught that the world is not evolving at the necessary pace. What are the challenges? Why has more meaningful progress not occurred, and faster?

Perhaps we can accelerate our progress through the intelligent use of technology. But *what* technology?

Technology of Life Itself

Humanity has participated in the creation, development, implementation, and use of many technologies throughout its history. Each of these advances has taken its place—to prolong life, speed its pace, or even to destroy it. Most were developed for the purpose of enhancing social well-being, born under a broad mission to "improve the standard of living." Some of these have yet to reveal their full implications.

When computers first became available, I thought they were complicated machines that were irrelevant to me. Today I use the computer to check my email at least twice a day. It is hard to imagine my life without this machine.

Technology that was once isolated in laboratories or monopolized by specialists now flows to all of us, a routine part of our daily lives. I am amazed at the speed with which it has altered our world, and I feel a humble gratitude for the extraordinary convenience it has provided us.

Still, I always return to the matter that has always been first and foremost in my heart: how to promote healthier living. Technology can speed the achievement of our intentions, but such acceleration is neutral with respect to the substance of those intentions. If we are vulnerable to harmful information, is it valuable for us to accelerate our exposure to negative ideas or images?

Technology is derived from the Greek, meaning "study of skills." Printing presses, steam engines, radio and television changed the course of our past. Today biotechnology and information technology are shaping the course of our future. But note that these technologies impact human experience through the filter of systems or specialists. However well-intentioned they may be, they are no substitute for individual judgment and responsibility.

What is needed are simple skills to upgrade life experience, that the individual herself can use responsibly without recourse to machines or institutions. Call these skills Human Technology (HT). *Human Technology is a toolkit for self-reliant management of the core issues of human life.* The core issues are health, sexuality, and life purpose. I contend that the skills of HT are the most important technology of all. They are the technologies of life itself. They lead to greater self-mastery and authentic living.

Let me share a story. A few months ago I met with a journalist who worked for a major national newspaper and was writing an in-depth story on health trends. While interviewing me, she mentioned she was suffering from severe and frequent bouts of gastrointestinal pain. She said that it actually prevented her from eating at least two days a week—particularly when she was on deadline. She related that she'd suffered with these symptoms for over three years. When I asked about managing the condition, her reply was that she simply took pills.

I pictured her modern, fast-paced, fully wired office with the latest laptop at her fingertips, just a keystroke away from accessing a mountain of health information. Multiple phones lines could connect her to dozens of health authorities. I imagined her ease and adeptness at using any one of these technologies.

I was also aware that practicing simple relaxation and breathing techniques and regularly stimulating certain acupressure points would be of great benefit to her. Even her doctor indicated that there was no significant problem with her intestines and that her symptoms were likely stress-related. He recommended that she create a more relaxed attitude and mind. Nevertheless, he gave her pain medication. Because this worked in the short term, she never seriously considered changing her life-style or resolving her problem through other means.

Although her life was surrounded by the greatest technology, both at work and from her doctor, I realized that she passively relied on her doctor to resolve her health problem. By not considering that she actually had "human technology" to manage her own health, she turned instead to the technology of medication.

I further realized that her medication habit was not the worst of it. More sadly, she did not even care that she was dependent on her pills. As far as she was concerned, she had everything: her career, her internet, and her pills. The gastrointestinal pains were a minor problem and had nothing to do with poor management, or lack of management, of anything.

Personally, I am troubled and occasionally angered by this kind of casual acceptance of dependency. From a health perspective, any doctor can tell you that most medicines can have undesirable side effects, and they may lose their efficacy after prolonged use. From an economic point of view, we all know that the cost of prescription drugs has become a major health care problem in the industrialized nations.

But let me tell you what saddens me most about this kind of casual pill-dependency. It represents a disconnection from our body and its wisdom. It is disrespectful of our magnificent innate potential for self-regulation and healing. *Accepting dependency signals a numbness to the true pulse of life itself.*

When we are sensitive and responsive to the signs and rhythms of our body, we are more deeply connected to the rich, wonderful texture of all life experience. Signals from the body —a butterfly in the stomach, a tingling in the toes, or even pains or discomforts—can take on meanings related to creative urges or spiritual growth. These sensations may even alert us to the state of our relationship with the earth itself. This kind of meaningfulness of our body sensations is difficult or impossible, if our sensory abilities have been dulled by apathy or medication dependence.

The burden of Human Technology is to stir you from apathy, and to give you some starter tools for your journey of authentic experience.

In retrospect, I consider all the methods and principles I have been teaching over the past twenty years as technologies. Unlike conventional "high" technology, HT is not intended to give us more time, allow us to work faster, or permit us to "stay connected" at every moment (although these benefits are also quite likely!). Instead, HT skills can be readily understood and applied, focusing on prevention and wellness rather than cures or symptoms.

Core HT Issues

I present the philosophy and practices of Human Technology as skills for three major life areas that we relate to virtually every day: common health concerns, sexuality, and life purpose. Neither the school, workplace, nor places of worship, are teaching the collective skills I present in this book.

Issues of health, sexuality, and life purpose have both personal and public dimensions. The industrialized nations are facing financial crises surrounding medical welfare programs. Cultural mores around sex can have a profound influence on an individual's sexuality. Awakening to our soul and life purpose is also a very personal and private matter with public consequences. A true understanding of the soul provides us with direction in our lives. The purpose of human life encompasses the human being not only as an individual, but also as a social being and participant in life's web. I firmly believe that those who engage in a sincere search for their life purpose will choose a life that realizes the highest, most profoundly social human values—love, compassion, harmony, and peace—and will aspire to make a positive, lasting contribution to their communities.

Self-Reliance: the Life of Creation

Are we currently living the best possible way? Is our life genuinely natural and humane? What do we need in order to improve our quality of life? Most importantly, who or what significantly influences our lives?

Nowadays many of us rely on institutions to help us deal with life's most basic issues. In some ways, we have traded our internal sense of judgment for systematized knowledge. Is this a good bargain?

We should ask ourselves these questions in the spirit of willingness to change. We are each, as individuals, uniquely responsible for the lives we live. There is no one else who should take responsibility for our choices. We may not be able to create or control all of the events that impact our lives but we can create and control our responses to *everything that we experience.*

Knowing the truth above does not mean that everyone is proactively creating their own life experience; in fact, too often the opposite is true. I do not believe that this result is due to a lack of desire. This is because many of us do not understand or use the principles and skills that would allow us to resolve our most basic life issues successfully. I believe this is an unintended and unrealized consequence of our overdependence on outside sources.

With the proliferation of increasingly complex technologies, society has become more specialized, which in turn has spurred it to become more systemized. As a result, we unknowingly let go of our authority even on matters closest to us, and instead have turned to specialists. This reliance on experts has permeated many parts of our lives: doctors and nutritionists tell us how to take care of our health and what to eat; child psychologists tell us how to raise our children, while school counselors tell us how to educate them. All of this has left most of us with a tendency to learn the minimum amount required to maintain a functional level of competence in those areas of our lives that have become specialized—from our personal lives to our societal experience.

Most of us have become detached from what being truly healthy means—individually, or as the collective that we call "society"—until our health is taken away from us in a dramatic moment of diagnosis by a specialist, or our collective health is threatened by the actions of terrorists, corporations, or governments. Then we want to do something immediately to correct the situation. Prevention, however, is not our primary mode of operation—it has remained a secondary part of our mindset.

Most of modern life seems to be designed so that we can adequately survive without facing the question of what true 'quality of life' means to us. Yet if we don't deeply explore this issue, our lives feel futile, and our time on earth could produce little in our experience that brings us inner peace, lasting joy— or anything of real intrinsic significance. We truly will be suffering "lives of quiet desperation."

We proliferate systems, institutions, and technologies

designed to produce a life of comfort and security. As systems have grown larger and more complex, we end up manipulating our lives to suit systems, rather than the other way around. Our overdependence on expert knowledge has led us to become less interested or even capable of looking beneath the surface of the grand technologies that are offered to us.

In the field of health care, we have come to believe that our bodies can only be analyzed, diagnosed, and serviced with the aid of computerized diagnostic equipment and other specialized devices. Awed by such complexity, many of us no longer try to understand for ourselves the majestic workings of the human body, *our* body. Too many of us are alienated from our bodies.

Even when we recognize that life-style choices have contributed to disease, there is too little effort to change. Instead, we turn to technological health care systems, which are designed to treat sickness only when it has reached grossly pathological stages. It is lamentable that we pay so little attention to preventative approaches to our health.

We are too often beholden to technology that is beyond our grasp—that is in the hands of experts. This is not as our lives were intended to be. Institutions or specialists cannot answer life's most important questions. This is solely the responsibility of the individual—the only being that can be held accountable for one's life.

The key to improving the quality of our lives is not found by making more convenient and perfect systems. By reaching into our HT toolkit, we will find skills which bring us back to our rightful place of mastery over technology and our lives at large. Systems can return to serving humanity, instead of reigning over us.

HT is designed to help us recover our power for self-reliance, to create lives well lived. I hope the HT toolkit becomes more intimately valuable to you, on a daily basis, than an MRI diagnosis, a computer, or any "complete" system of teaching.

2

Self-Reliance for Health

WHEN YOU FEEL LIKE you are coming down with the flu, what do you do? Do you go to the drugstore and buy an over-the-counter medication? Or do you go to the hospital? Or, knowing that there is not a cure for the flu, do you prefer to wait for the virus to run its course? Do you regret not having gotten vaccinated prior to the "flu season"?

As a parent, you have probably had the experience of staying up all night tending to a child with a burning fever. You have probably also seen a family member suffer for days with a bad cold, wishing you could help in some way. During these times, my hope is that you will have methods to help that you can use with confidence, that do not require medication or complicated expertise.

Health is something that is best maintained by oneself on a daily basis. In order to do this, one must have a clear and intimate understanding of the basic principle of how health is maintained in the body. By intimate, I do not mean an intellectual understanding. Rather, we must know our own bodies like we would know a loved one.

Taking care of ourselves, being in charge of our lives, is a way of saying we are worthwhile, an acknowledgement of our self-worth. We must awaken to the many inherent sensibilities and sensitivities of our body, and be able to feel when we are moving towards health or away from it.

The first principle we must understand is our innate healing power. Our role as masters of our bodies is to facilitate and enhance this process with the tools of Human Technology. I believe we should try to maximize the natural healing mechanisms of the human body when we feel unwell.

Specifically, the HT perspective on health stresses two other points. First, disease can result from an imbalance of life-energy (Ki) in the body. We will talk more about this in the next chapter. Secondly, we must remember that our actions and life-style choices act directly to either optimize our health or undermine it. Nothing compares to the well-being that results when healthy habits are maintained. Please consider your health in all its dimensions: energy circulation, physical conditioning, mental and emotional well-being, and social health. These are the foundation for our quality of life.

Acquiring Health Management Skills

Some people, even with significant physical limitations, still strive with determined will to fulfill their life purpose. However, they tend to be the heroic few. For many people, physical or mental illness brings hardships not only to themselves but also to those around them, ultimately distorting their character and their relationships. Those with experience know that it is very hard to maintain a happy home if someone in the family is seriously ill. Yet health is not important solely to the individual or the family. It is also a societal and national issue. Staying healthy may mean avoiding chronic diseases that can limit our productivity or our ability to fully participate in societal affairs.

Health care now plays a large role in national economies. In developed countries, medical expenditures comprise roughly 10 percent of our total economic activity (Gross Domestic Product). In the United States in the year 2005, this number has risen to 14 percent, partly as a result of higher prescription drug costs and advances in medical technology. Are these monies being well spent?

I propose that we all acquire *health management skills* that have a low risk of side effects, that are effective, inexpensive, and easily learned and used. The HT toolkit contains these skills. To benefit individuals and families, I would like to help make Human Technology methods widely available.

Turning our Approach "Inside Out"

Do we have enough confidence and skills to take care of the majority of our health concerns? Some people think that it is not possible to manage their health without the help of advanced technology. Deep down, however, most of us know that we all have the resources we need to care for our basic needs. Sustained health can be our normal condition. This is the first change in mindset that is required for us to fully explore the potential of the methods of Human Technology.

Human Technology is about turning our lives "inside out." Currently, it is "outside in," and that reversal is unhealthy.

When I say that for many people life is "outside in," I mean that life can be seen as a series of events occurring outside of oneself —events which impact or determine the course of personal experience. Logically, one then looks outside again to bring in whatever seems to be needed to face those events.

In the case of health, this thinking may lead us to assume that an outside source is required for healing. We may reflexively turn to a counselor, doctor or specialist to solve our problem.

If we knew how extraordinary our brains are and our capacity for self-healing, our first instinct would be for self-reliance. We would seek solutions from within.

That is what Human Technology is all about. It is about bringing us closer to personal mastery by turning our lives "inside out." It is about providing an awareness that we have the tools we will need to live a rich, full, and rewarding life—and that those tools are within us.

Health management based on Human Technology is about learning simple, natural self-care methods to prevent and treat common illnesses, thereby managing most daily health concerns. Our breathing, our body itself, and the life-energy which flows through us, become tools we can use once we understand the principles by which they work, and the basic skills for applying those principles.

Life need not occur as an experience that is happening TO us. It can be an experience that is happening *through* us. We can place ourselves in charge. In fact, we always *are* "in charge." HT is intended to provide the tools which can make our mastery a reality.

In the following chapters, I will discuss the basic principles and skills for health management, which will include breathing, meditation, acupuncture/acupressure, and moxibustion. The fundamentals of these topics are straightforward and easy to understand. Without formal training, you can use most of these skills for yourself and others in your family.

When I spoke at the beginning of this book about modern technology, I mentioned the home computer. Many people have had the experience of being perplexed when facing an error message on their monitor that abruptly stops them in the midst of an operation. They bring in a computer specialist, or call a technical support person to get the machine up and running again.

Often what the technician directs us to do is laughably simple, and after their instructions we no longer are perplexed. Indeed, we come to wonder how we could ever have been confused or uncertain about what to do in those situations.

You are about to find out that it is exactly the same with Human Technology as it is with computer technology. It is not nearly as complex or complicated as it seems when looking from the "outside in." So, now let us turn everything "inside out," and take a look at some basic principles of health.

3

The Core of Health

CLASSICAL TRADITIONS OF MEDICINE, both Greek and Oriental, described the natural world as a composition of fundamental elements including Water, Fire, Earth, and Air. (Oriental traditions included Wood and Metal in place of Air.)

Descriptions of the qualities and actions of these elements were based on many generations of observations by agricultural civilizations, which were keenly tuned to the relationships between humanity, earth, and the cosmos. They are the result of simple and intuitive observations of reality. Though today we may choose to consider these elements symbols or metaphors, it can still be highly useful to understand our health in terms of these dynamic primordial qualities.

Let us begin by taking earth and air as the base. Then, fire and water are the elements that create balance and harmony. The highest order that the harmonious balance of water and fire creates is the phenomenon that we call life. Life emerges from the right amount of water and heat, evolving to a higher order. To maintain life, air (breathing oxygen) and earth (consuming nutrients) are required. Health is a dynamic order that requires balancing these four elements. When one has an optimal mix, we call this a healthy state. When balance is absent and the system has less order, we call this a diseased state.

In any life form, the balance of water and fire is crucial to health. Conversely, an imbalance of fire and water is a primary cause of disease.

Spontaneously, fire rises up and water runs down—think of rising hot air or falling rain. This seems perfectly natural. This shows the direction of energy flow toward the increase of entropy (increasing randomness and disorder). However, this is only half of the story.

Water Up, Fire Down

There is another, equally natural, yet fundamentally different flow in which water goes up and fire comes down. This flow creates miracles of the spontaneous decrease of entropy.

It is called Su-seung-hwa-gang, which means "Water Up, Fire Down"—water energy ascends while fire energy descends. By overcoming entropy (disorder), this flow culminates in the expression of life itself.

We can readily observe examples of Su-seung-hwa-gang. Think about the cycle of water on earth. When the fire energy of the sun shines down on the earth, the water energy of rivers, lakes, and oceans rises to form clouds.

Or, consider how plants obtain their energy. Plants receive fire energy from the sun shining down on their leaves, while drawing the water energy up through their roots from moisture in the ground. With this cycle of energy, plants and trees grow and bear fruit. In the winter, when the ground is too frozen for plants to draw water up, leaves fall to the ground and no fruit is produced. Life itself goes into dormancy until the natural cycle of energy is once again possible.

Su-seung-hwa-gang is the core principle for human health. When the human body is in balance, the cool water energy travels upward toward the head along the back side of the body, while the hot fire energy flows down the front side of the body to the lower abdomen. This constitutes a complete cycle of energy circulation. By repeating this circulation, life maintains its balance and continuity. Perhaps you have heard the expressions, "I have a fire in my belly," or "Keep a cool head."

The organs facilitating this natural circulation are the kidneys and heart with the help of our bodies' energy center called the Dahn-jon, located approximately two inches below our navel and two inches inward. The kidneys generate water energy

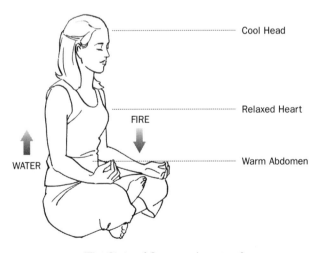

[The State of Su-seung-hwa-gang]

in the human body, while the heart generates fire energy. When our energy flow is smooth and balanced, the Dahn-jon imparts heat to the kidneys and sends the water energy up. This cools the brain and brings down the heat in the heart so that fire energy moves downward. When the water energy travels upward along the spine, the brain feels cool and refreshed. When the fire energy flows down from the chest, the lower abdomen and intestines become warm and flexible. In this cycle of energy flow, the Dahn-jon, the energy center in the lower abdomen, performs the most crucial function.

If the energy flow is reversed and fire energy moves upward while water energy moves downward, then your abdomen may be clammy and your neck and shoulders stiff. You may feel "weak at heart" or fatigue. In this state, many people experience problems with digestion, including chronic constipation and tenderness in the lower abdomen, or circulatory problems.

There are two common reasons for improper action of Su-seung-hwa-gang. The first occurs when the Dahn-jon, which acts to draw in and store energy, is too weak or inefficient to do its job properly. In this case, intellectual activity will result in fire energy moving upward to the brain.

The second is stress, which has a negative effect on the downward flow of energy through the chest. When this flow is blocked, energy backs up and returns to the head, resulting in anxiety and nervousness.

In our bodies, when "Water Up, Fire Down" is in effect, our lower abdomen is warm while our head is cool. Our hands and feet are warm while we have plenty of saliva within our mouths. We perceive with greater clarity of sight and hearing. We feel positive and relaxed. In such an upbeat state, we are inclined to think positively and creatively.

The state of Su-seung-hwa-gang facilitates better functioning of all other organ systems. This state is the normative goal of all health-related methods of Human Technology. Proper breathing, meditation, meridian exercises, acupuncture, acupressure, and moxibustion are all essentially techniques to create the flow of "Water Up, Fire Down" in our bodies.

WATER UP, FIRE DOWN (Healthy State)	FIRE UP, WATER DOWN (Unhealthy State)
Circulation, dynamic, liveliness	Disconnection, static, lifelessness
Sweet saliva in the mouth	Dry mouth, bitter taste
Warm hands and feet	Cold hands and feet
Cool and refreshed head	Heat and pain in the head
Warm abdomen filled with energy	Abdomen lacks warmth and energy
Regular bowel movements	Constipation, digestive problems
One feels refreshed and energized	One feels tired and uncomfortable

[Water Up, Fire Down *vs* Fire Up, Water Down]

4

Back to Your Breath and Body

THERE ARE MANY EFFECTIVE METHODS OF HEALING that can be categorized as Human Technology. We can make use of a variety of approaches including breath-work, meditation, exercise, diet, and dance, to bring balance to our bodies and minds. Of these, breath-work may be the simplest method. This is because breathing is something that everyone does. It is not a question of whether you do it, but how.

Respiration takes place in a cycle of four steps: inhalation, rest, exhalation, and then pause. In breathing, we feel most comfortable when we exhale and our breathing stops for a moment before we inhale, and we feel least comfortable when we inhale and then hold our breath before exhaling.

The way we breathe can be an indicator of the level of emotional or physical well-being that we are experiencing in that moment. Conversely, we can actually produce well-being through our breath. Just breathing correctly can help us a great deal in maintaining our health. "Good breathing" is the most basic of basics. I have seen many cases in which a person's health was restored just by correcting the breathing.

Many scientists now agree that chronic stress responses can lead to disease. Although some situations and environments produce more stress than others, it is always helpful to remember the tools that any individual can use, whatever the stress level of their circumstances. Our stress responses can be improved by strengthening our skills at regulating our emotions or governing the mind. Correct breathing enables us to better direct our minds, so it is critical for optimal health.

There is scarcely a person who does not know that the best way to quickly temper anger, decrease frustration, and calm jittery nerves is to simply stop everything and "take a deep breath."

How you breathe, and whether you give yourself a chance to "consciously breathe" every day, can strongly influence your state of health. The breath is a simple but powerful part of our HT toolkit.

Which Comes First—Inhaling or Exhaling?

Consider the following question for a moment. Does life begin by breathing in or out? We cannot really remember this ourselves, but witnessing childbirth allows us to confirm that life begins with exhalation. We let out a great cry when we are born, "Waaa!" This is the beginning of an exhalation. By emptying its lungs of the small breath it holds, the baby leaves room for air to enter, becoming connected with nature's great current of life.

In the Korean language, the word, Ho-heup (which means respiration or breathing) has both physiological and philosophical significance. Ho means breathing out, and Heup means breathing in. We need to pay attention to the fact that this com-pound word is Ho-heup, not Heup-ho. This signifies that breathing out comes first, not breathing in.

Life begins by emptying oneself. The rhythm of life starts when we have emptied ourselves and then allow that empty place to be filled. When I let go of something small (the small breath I hold on to), I gain something great (the atmosphere of nature). This understanding, also applied to our "small think-ing," can lead to enlightenment.

Now, let us examine death. Does life end with an inhalation or an exhalation? If you have witnessed a death, you may have noticed that many people stop breathing after inhaling one last time. Although this could be explained in various ways, we might simply say that the body has an instinctive mechanism by which it tries to maintain life as long as it has even a little strength left.

Inhaling takes energy, while exhaling does not require much energy at all. Try breathing a few times and you will see what I mean. A breath taken is exhaled naturally. On account of this, as long as we are strong enough, we try to breathe in again because of our attachment to life. This explains why in most cases life ends with an inhalation.

It feels stuffy to stop in the middle of inhalation. This means that for many people, dying is not a very pleasant experience. Dying on an inhaled breath means dying in struggle and often pain. In contrast, when people are absolutely satisfied with what they have done through their lives, when they are totally sure of the continuity of their existence, then I think they will be more likely to exhale. Their experience of death will be that much more pleasant. So please remember the proper way of breathing, even at the moment of death—just in case.

Breathing Your Way to Health

Breath-work is really very easy; so we do not need to "over-think" it. Simply watching and focusing on our respiration, following along with its natural rhythms, causes our breathing to deepen automatically. Very few people, however, take the time to do this. Breathing has become so automatic that some people go through their entire lives and never use the mechanism of breathing *intentionally*—that is, in a certain way, on purpose, at least once a day.

There is a close correlation between depth of respiration and health. Our breathing is deeper when we are younger and becomes shallower with age. We observe that newborn children breathe with their abdomen, their lower belly rising and falling. The center of breathing gradually rises as children grow older. This change proceeds from what is called "abdominal breathing" to "chest breathing," and then to "shoulder breathing."

If you watch people of advanced age, or patients who are seriously ill, you will see that their shoulders rise and fall as they breathe. This indicates how shallow their respiration has become. In Korean, the shallowest respiration is called Mok-sum, or "throat breathing." When respiration becomes shallower than this, a person dies. His or her Mok-sum, or "throat breathing," is cut off.

Breath-work is a simple discipline that allows us to train ourselves to breathe in a certain way, essentially to keep our breathing naturally deep. As a basic principle, respiration should be deep, light, and natural. Breathing that is natural, and yet deep and light, is healthy. It may seem that breathing both deeply and lightly is contradictory. We associate deepness with heaviness, and connect lightness with shallowness. This principle of deepness and lightness might seem at odds with itself. How is such breathing possible?

The Master Tool

Deep breathing occurs naturally if we breathe with our awareness focused on our Dahn-jon, which you may remember is the Korean name for our bodies' energy center. It is located roughly two inches below the navel and two inches inside the body, in the center of the abdomen.

As you do your breath-work, focus your mind's attention on this area of your body. Feel your lower abdomen rising when you breathe in and falling when you breathe out. Do this slowly and concentrate on your breathing. If this method seems difficult, place one hand on your lower abdomen and the other on your chest. As you breathe, feel the hand on your lower abdomen moving while the hand on your chest stays still.

If you take time to do this daily, soon your mind will do it automatically—it will simply become part of how you breathe. One part of your mind will do this deep breathing, while you focus on other things that allow you to move through your day. This approach is called Dahn-jon breathing.

Dahn-jon breathing is closely related to the movement of the diaphragm, a dome-shaped structure that assists in breathing and acts as a natural partition between our heart and lungs on the one hand, and our stomach, spleen, pancreas, liver, kidneys, bladder, and small and large intestines on the other.

When we breathe deeply, our diaphragm moves downward as we inhale and upward as we exhale. The more the diaphragm moves, the more our lungs are able to expand, which means that more oxygen can be taken in and more carbon dioxide released with each breath.

The diaphragm is attached to the lower rib cage and has strands extending to the lumbar vertebrae. When we breathe fully and deeply, the belly, lower rib cage, and lower back expand on inhalation, thus pushing the diaphragm down deeper into the abdomen. The same structures retract on exhalation. In deep Dahn-jon breathing, these rhythmic movements help to detoxify our inner organs, promote blood flow and peristalsis, and pump fluid more efficiently through our lymphatic system.

Dahn-jon breathing can allow breathing to become natural and deep. But how can breathing become light? Our respiration becomes lighter if we breathe with a heart full of joy and gratitude. Thanking our bodies when we inhale and thanking earth when we exhale causes a smile to form naturally on our lips. Breathing becomes as light as a feather, all on its own. Easy!

Using Breath to Control the Mind

Our emotional or mental states have various ways of manifesting themselves in the body. Some of these are body temperature, pulse, blood pressure, respiration, complexion, and brain waves. Of these phenomena that reveal our condition, respiration differs in character from the others.

As I have said, respiration occurs naturally, whether we are aware of it or not. Unlike some other bodily systems, however, we can control it consciously, even though it is monitored by the autonomic nervous system. (You can also learn to bring your blood pressure down, lower your pulse rate, and even alter your brain waves, but not as easily as controlling your breath!)

Our bodies and minds are closely interconnected. Our state of mind is expressed in physical phenomena, and, conversely, physical phenomena reflect our state of mind. It is a two-way street. By controlling our bodies, we can change our state of mind. With sufficient awareness of our mind, we can more easily alter our physical experience.

Breathing can be used as an important tool to direct the mind. When we are emotionally agitated, it is difficult to use our best judgment. In such circumstances, we can make mistakes involving important issues. Or, without a complete view of our situation, we can cause "accidents." When caught in the throes of emotion, we can avoid many mistakes or accidents if we just take three deep breaths. What is amazing is that nearly everyone knows this, but very few of us use this knowledge.

I believe that a habit of good breathing can prevent much unhappiness. So, if you become emotionally upset, do not try to analyze your situation by thinking. Instead, focus on your breathing. This is much easier and more effective. Stop thinking for a moment and concentrate on your breathing. Deep breathing will quiet your emotions and enable you to better assess your circumstances.

Now, that is such a simple suggestion that you may just have read right over it. So please allow me to repeat it.

I believe that a habit of good breathing can prevent much unhappiness. So, if you become emotionally upset, do not try to analyze your situation by thinking. Instead, focus on your breathing.

Taking a Breath of Fresh Air

We have all heard the phrase, "She is like a breath of fresh air" or, "Let's let in some fresh air."

There is nothing like a breath of fresh air! Everyone loves it!

No one ever says "no" to a breath of fresh air. There is nothing like it to wake people up, to stimulate them, to get them going again. All that we need to do to stay physically healthy and mentally alert is allow the fresh air in and let the toxins out. That is all breathing is about. When we breathe in, we take in fresh air. When we breathe out, we release the toxins. In medicine, our in-breath is called "inspiration," and our out-breath is called "expiration."

Now, I want you to consider something that you may never have conceptualized or imagined before.

Thoughts are the breath of the brain.

Just as we take air into our bodies, we are also allowing thoughts to be processed by our brains.

Breathing is mechanical. You do not have to think about breathing, and you do not have to make yourself do it. It is an automatic action of the body. Breathing happens by itself. It is what the body does.

Thinking is also mechanical. You do not have to think about thinking, and you do not have to make yourself do it. It is a routine of the brain. Thinking happens by itself. It is what the brain does.

Of course, how the body breathes is another matter. That is something you can control—although very few people do. And how the brain thinks is another matter. That is something you can control—although very few people do.

Meditation and Why the Brain Loves It

Meditation is the brain's way of "breathing deeply." It is Dahn-jon breathing for the brain!

Now, remember that the mind and the body are inextricably

linked. And just as Dahn-jon breathing calms the mind, so, too, does meditation calm the body.

Meditation is a term that refers both to a state of consciousness in which a practitioner watches oneself, as well as a method for achieving such a state.

As a method, meditation means quieting the mind in order to more clearly see one's self. That is something that most people know. But here is something that many people do not realize: meditation is a phenomenon that occurs naturally as our consciousness awakens.

Ultimately, meditation is simply self-watching from a different aspect of consciousness—a way of becoming selfless. This you can do while washing dishes, walking the dog, mowing the lawn, or making a meal. In fact, preparing a meal with love is a wonderful meditation.

HT meditation focuses on being here now. It means being fully present in this moment. It means being aware of everything that is or is not going on in this moment. The present is not tomorrow nor is it yesterday. There is nothing present except exactly what is occurring right now.

After attaining awareness of this moment, meditation further entails separating ourselves from that. It constitutes observing yourself and looking at the moment you are living and saying, "This is not me. This is mine. I created this, but I am not this. I am the creator of it and the watcher of it, but I am not that which is being watched."

This is knowing who you really are, and it is the aim and the result of HT meditation. It is the brain's experience of "breathing deeply." From a neural perspective, I believe that meditation is an expansion of consciousness to the unconscious realm. This means that consciousness escapes the exclusive domain of knowledge and the five senses, and that it penetrates the boundaries between the neocortex (responsible for higher thinking) and limbic system (responsible for emotions) in the brain. Ultimately, I believe it is possible to unlock and become one with the unconscious mind with full awareness. I have experienced this subjectively, and I hope one day that neuroscientists can explain it objectively.

I suggest that becoming one with the unconscious in an awakened state is one form of enlightenment. We awaken to our true essence and we become aware of our "oneness." After having such an experience, it becomes possible to watch the realm of consciousness from within the unconscious. We are able to see things as they really are, without the filter of thoughts or ideas. This is called "detached watching."

As a tool of HT, our most fundamental meditation practice combines Dahn-jon breathing with Ji-gam (energy sensitivity training). The interplay between the development of our energy sensitivity and watchfulness of our thoughts and breath allows us to quiet our minds and simply be in the moment.

The training I present below helps us reach a state of relaxed concentration very fast. We are able to learn a way to become present in the here and now by concentrating on the breath that leaves and enters our bodies and the subtle sensations of the body's energy.

The key to meditation is to extend this state of relaxed concentration, creating a peaceful and clear consciousness of being, here and now. It is this state that we wish to bring to our every day lives.

Energy Sensitivity Training

1. Sit on a chair or in half-lotus position on the floor and straighten your back.
2. Place your hands on your knees with your palms facing

up and close your eyes. Relax your body, especially your neck and shoulders. Relax your mind. Inhale deeply, and let go of any remaining tension while exhaling. (Soft meditative music in the background may be helpful.)

3. Raise your hands slowly to chest level, with your palms facing each other but not touching. First concentrate on any sensation you may feel between your palms. At first, you may feel warmth in your hands, but you will soon feel your own pulse.

4. Now, put about two to four inches of space in between your hands and concentrate fully on the space. Imagine that your shoulders, arms, wrists, and hands are floating in a vacuum, weightless.

5. Pull your hands apart and push them closer in again as you maintain your concentration. You might feel a tingling sensation of electricity, a magnetic attraction pulling your hands toward each other, or pushing your hands apart. You might even feel as if you are holding a soft cotton ball between your hands, or moving slowly through warm water. All these feelings are a manifestation of your energy flow.

6. When the sensation becomes more real, pull your hands

     farther apart or push them closer together. The sensation
     will not go away but will expand and become stronger.
7.   Breathe in and out slowly and deeply three times.
8.   Rub your hands together briskly until warm, and gently
     caress your eyes, face, neck, and chest.

When you try this training, at first, the feeling might be very
subtle. Never mind. Hold on to that sensation with all your
concentration and sincerity. That feeling is there. It is real. It is
an actual physical manifestation. However, because it may be
very subtle, you may think that you are imagining it. Keep practicing and soon you will sense the energy more strongly.
Awakening this innate sensitivity will bring you a new dimension to self-reliance for health.

Meridian Exercises

Human Technology suggests that meditative experience can be
deeper if preceded by stimulation and energizing our bodies
and breath. We do this through "meridian exercises," an effective way of moving our bodies to improve our breath-work and
to enhance our awareness while energizing our bodies.

    The meridian system of the body is a series of channels or
pathways running from the feet to the head and the head to the
hands transporting Ki (Qi or Chi). Ki is usually described as the
life-energy that is associated with all living processes in Oriental
Medicine. It flows through all life forms. Meridians can be
likened to rivers of the body. The meridian system is responsible for the distribution of Ki throughout its intricate network,
nourishing and influencing body, mind, and spirit. Acupressure
(or acupuncture) points, which are distributed along meridians,

are portals through which energy enters and exits the body.

It is easy to understand the system of meridians and acupressure points if you imagine the body as representing land. The meridians would be the main roads while the acupressure points are the bus stops. Just as goods and merchandise are transported across a highway system, our body can supply energy to the organs and different parts of the body through meridians. If energy flows well through the meridians, it is distributed evenly throughout the body, helping the body and brain to maintain their optimal conditions.

Our body consists of twelve main meridians and eight secondary meridians. The twelve main meridians are each associated with a principle internal organ and are named accordingly. These twelve meridians run on both sides, symmetrically on either side of the body. Energy flows constantly through them.

Meridian exercises are designed to open the meridian system of the body, and to balance the energy of their associated organs. Meridian exercises combine proper breathing with stretching movements. When breath is combined with body movement, metabolism can be influenced more effectively.

While there are hundreds of meridian exercises, as an HT tool this book will introduce several fundamental ones for maintaining our health. Whole Body Patting, Toe Tapping, Intestinal Exercises, and Abdominal Clapping are ideal for your morning and evening routine. I believe that consistent practice of meridian exercises can help maintain our health in the optimal state.

WHOLE BODY PATTING

This exercise consists of patting the body to help circulation, open blockages, and release stagnant energy throughout the whole body. By patting, cells are strengthened as they are stimulated and acupressure points are opened. All age groups can do this exercise. It is a very effective method for general health. Pat the body gently and comfortably to achieve the desired results. You can concentrate better if you allow your eyes to follow your movements.

1.   Stand with your legs shoulder-width apart. Form your fingers into stiff claws and lightly tap all over your head and face.
2.   Stretch out your left arm with your palm facing up. Take your right hand and starting from the left shoulder, pat rhythmically downward all the way to the left hand.
3.   Then turn your left hand over and with your right hand, pat your way back up to the left shoulder again.
4.   Repeat step 2 and step 3 with the opposite hand.
5.   Pat your chest with both hands.

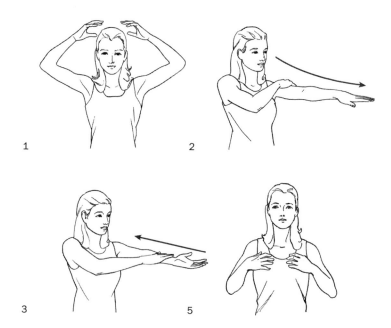

6. Starting from your chest, pat your ribs, abdomen, and sides.
7. With both hands, pat the area just below the right rib cage where your liver is located and concentrate on radiating positive, clear energy to the liver.
8. With both hands, tap the area just below the left rib cage where your stomach is located and concentrate on radiating positive, clear energy to your stomach.
9. Bend over slightly from the waist, and pat the area on your lower back (on both sides) where your kidneys are located and move up, tapping as far as your hands can reach. Then tap your way down to your buttocks.

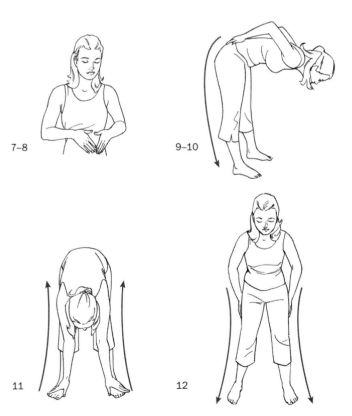

7–8   9–10

11   12

10. Starting from your buttocks, pat your way down the back of your legs to your ankles.

11. From the ankles, start patting your way up the front of your legs until you reach your thighs.

12. From your upper thighs, pat your way down the outsides of your legs to your ankles.

13. From the ankles, pat your way up the insides of your legs to your upper thighs.

14. Finish up by striking your lower abdomen about twenty times. This exercise is most effective when done with the legs shoulder-width apart with the knees slightly bent.

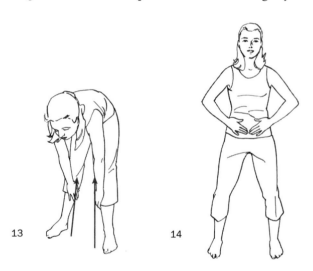

13   14

TOE TAPPING

This exercise helps circulation to the lower extremities and balances water and fire energy in your body. It will also help provide a deeper and more peaceful sleep. You can perform this exercise from either a lying or sitting position. If lying down place your hands on your abdomen and move your toes side to side, tapping the big toes together and the pinky toes on the floor. Keep your heels together throughout the exercise. Begin with one hundred times and increase to five hundred times.

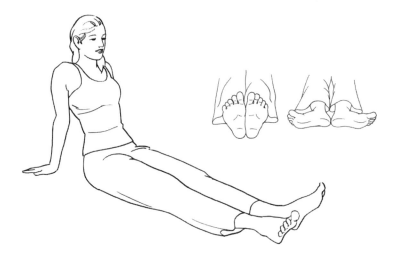

ABDOMINAL CLAPPING

Abdominal Clapping is a simple but effective method for strengthening the lower abdomen (especially Dahn-jon, your body's energy center) by rhythmically striking (patting) it with the palms of both hands. Stimulating the area in this way facilitates the circulation of both blood and energy throughout the body. You will also feel increased warmth in the area. This exercise will assist in the prompt removal of excess gases and waste from the body.

1. Spread your feet shoulder-width apart and bend your knees slightly.
2. Point your toes slightly inward and feel a slight tightening of the lower abdomen.

3. Strike the lower abdomen area with both palms in rhythm, lightly bouncing your knees with each strike.
4. Begin with only fifty strikes per session and work up to three hundred strikes as the lower abdomen is strengthened. You may increase the number and force of the strikes with more practice.

INTESTINAL EXERCISES

Intestinal Exercise refers to the rhythmic pulling in and pushing out of the abdominal wall, which stimulates the intestines. This exercise will increase the flexibility of the intestines and facilitate efficient circulation of both energy and blood. If you also tighten your rectal muscles during this exercise, you will be able to gather energy and feel warmth much more quickly. However, you should not overdo this exercise in the beginning, as it may result in some discomfort.

1. This exercise can be performed standing up or lying down. When standing up, assume the same position as

the abdominal clapping position (knees slightly bent, toes turned slightly inward). When lying down, lie on your back with your legs shoulder-width apart. Form a triangle by touching your thumbs and forefingers together, and place them lightly on the lower abdomen.

2. When pulling in, pull as if the front wall of your abdomen is trying to touch your back. Tighten your rectal muscles at the same time.

3. Then, as if sucking air out of a balloon, push your lower abdomen out slightly, until you feel outward pressure in your lower abdomen.

4. Start with one set of fifty and work your way up to a set of three hundred as you advance.

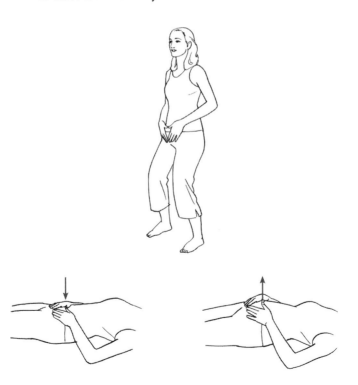

For the Lungs and Large Intestine

1. Stand with your feet shoulder-width apart and lock your fingers behind you.
2. While exhaling, bend your upper trunk forward with your face toward your knees. Stretch both arms backwards and up.
3. Inhale calmly when your body has stretched to its limit, and keep this position for a while. You may feel some tension in the lower legs, stomach, back, shoulders, or arms.
4. Exhale calmly so that you can release any tension, similar to relaxing your attention.
5. Repeat step 3 and step 4 several times.

For the Spleen and Stomach

1. Place your left foot forward. Inhale. Raise your left hand towards the ceiling as you tilt your body backwards, following the movement of your hand with your eyes.
2. Simultaneously, place weight on your right foot with your right hand on your right thigh. Tilt backwards as

much as you can. Exhale, and return to step 1. Notice the sensations in your lower abdomen and waist as they become stimulated.

3. Repeat twice. Then perform steps 1 through 3 using the opposite side of the body.

FOR THE LIVER AND GALL BLADDER

1. Sit up with your spine straight and spread your legs as wide as you can. With your right hand grab your right ankle. Bend from the waist as you bring your left hand over to your right foot. Hold for as long as is comfortable while focusing on stretching your left side and thighs as much as possible.

2. Repeat on the opposite side. Repeat each side at least twice.

FOR THE HEART AND SMALL INTESTINE

1. Sit in half-lotus posture and lock your fingers behind your neck. Inhale. Bend your upper body forward and touch the floor with your forehead.
2. Hold this posture for as long as you comfortably can. Exhale and expand your chest as you return to your original posture.

FOR THE KIDNEY AND BLADDER

1. From a comfortable sitting position straighten your legs, stretching them forward, with your feet next to each other. Pull your toes back toward your body so that your ankles form a 90-degree angle. From this position, bend your upper body forward and grab your ankles with your hands.
2. Perform the movements slowly, matching them to your breathing. Exhale as you bend your body forward and inhale as you raise it up again. When you bend your

upper body forward, also bend your neck forward, and grab your ankles with your hands. Be careful not to overdo it; you will know you have if your body tightens up. Adjust the exercise to your flexibility level.

We each have certain tools that are critical to doing our job, whether we are plumbers, carpenters, engineers, athletes, doctors, or in the case of this book, human beings. The tools that I have introduced in this chapter form the foundation of the self-care health methods in our HT toolkit.

The power of these tools lies in their simplicity. Whether through breath-work, meditation, or meridian exercises, all we need is our sincere attention and our bodies.

As I said, Human Technology is not as complicated as you may have imagined!

5

A Healing Trio: Acupuncture, Acupressure, and Moxibustion

By using three basic Human Technology techniques that activate the body's natural healing capacity—acupuncture, acupressure, and moxibustion—we can prevent and treat many common health problems. Amazingly, all we have to do is stimulate our internal healing mechanism—almost like turning on a switch.

Practiced on specific response points on the human body, acupuncture, acupressure, and moxibustion have long been foundational to the healing arts in northeast Asia. In acupuncture, a thin needle is inserted into response points. Acupressure is pressure applied to the same points using the fingers or tools. Moxibustion is the practice of burning small, tightly rolled dried cones of the plant mugwort on or over specific points.

In 1976, the World Health Organization (WHO) recognized acupuncture as a legitimate practice. After exhaustive scientific study, WHO declared in 1998 that acupuncture is an appropriate treatment for 300 common illnesses, and recommended that acupuncture be used as a diagnostic tool.

Acupuncturists must undergo training and receive a license in order to practice in the United States, the United Kingdom, France, and Germany, among other countries.

In the United States, the first state licenses for acupuncture were issued in the mid-1970s in California. Not all states regulate acupuncture. Since acupuncture is a relatively new profession in the industrialized countries, there is wide variation in licensing, training, guidelines for practice, and proficiency examinations from state to state.

At the time of this writing, in New Mexico acupuncturists have significant latitude in their practice of acupuncture. Upon licensure they are granted the title of Doctor of Oriental Medicine. By contrast, the states of Idaho and Wyoming have no acupuncture provisions; practicing acupuncture is neither legal nor illegal. In Arizona, one can self-administer acupuncture without a license.

Since state licensing procedures vary greatly, it is best to check local regulations by contacting the department of public health in your state government, so that you understand whether it is legal to self-administer acupuncture to family members. (Acupressure, which is discussed later in this chapter, can be an effective alternative to acupuncture, and does not typically require a license.)

In the West, moxibustion is not as widely known as acupuncture and acupressure. In general, the effects of moxibustion can be long-term and stable, when practiced consistently. Also, it is very easy to use. Thus it is particularly valuable for preventive care and health maintenance.

Fire and Water in Acupuncture and Moxibustion

As we discussed in Chapter 3 (The Core of Health), Oriental Medicine suggests that life is generated and maintained by the harmony and balance between two primordial elements: Fire and Water. One reason that acupuncture and moxibustion are effective is that these techniques are methods that affect the balance between fire and water—moxibustion affects fire, and acupuncture water.

Oriental Medicine posits the existence of five primordial elements: Wood, Fire, Earth, Metal, and Water. These elements emerge in physical reality as the result of the interactions of the two fundamental poles of the universe: Yin and Yang.

The five elements have either generative or controlling properties with respect to one another. In the order of the generative cycle, the five elements can be ordered thus: Water–Wood–Fire–Earth–Metal, and returning to Water. In terms of the controlling cycle, the five elements can be ordered as follows: Metal–Wood–Earth–Water–Fire, and returning to Metal.

For example, water nourishes growth of a tree (wood); wood generates fire; fire creates ashes that turn to earth; and earth over time produces metal (ores). Conversely, metal cuts wood; wood controls the earth (tree roots); earth blocks the flow of water; water can extinguish fire; and fire melts metal.

In this chain of relationships, acupuncture has the characteristics of Metal while moxibustion represents Wood. In the generative cycle, Metal can increase Water energy while Wood can increase Fire energy. Depending upon the duration, direction, and intensity of the treatment, one can either relieve an overflowing condition or tonify the missing element.

Although some treatments can become complex when studied professionally, simple stimulation at the major points is usu-

ally enough to serve as useful treatment for minor injuries or as
a preventative measure.

Trigger Points: Inspiring the Brain to Heal the Body

A major reason why acupuncture and moxibustion are not
more widely understood is that biomedicine tends to take a
reductive approach to health. Analyzing acupuncture or moxibustion as purely physical inputs cannot explain their treatment
effects. If one analyzes these practices this way, an acupuncture
needle is just a thin piece of stainless steel, and moxibustion will
look like a pulp of dried leaves (mugwort) without pharmaco-
logical properties. The acupuncture needle or moxibustion pulp
themselves are not doing the healing—they function only as
keys to activate the healing processes of the body. And what
controls these processes? Yes, the human brain!

The brain is connected to sensors all over the body, which
manage its natural healing processes. When the appropriate sig-
nal is received at certain places, the brain initiates healing mechanisms, mostly triggered and controlled by hormones. The sensor locations are called response points or acupuncture points.
In my native language, Korean, we call these Kyung-hyuls. They
are gates on our bodies through which energy comes and goes;
they are also energy storage and distribution points.

Meridians are the paths along which energy travels in our
bodies. It may be helpful to think of Meridians as corporeal bus
routes and acupuncture points as bus stations. Acupuncture
points are points on the body, locations where water and fire
can be controlled most effectively, at which a major response
can be elicited by a small amount of energy. You could consider
an acupuncture point as a strategic location, such as where a

dam would need to be constructed to control the level of water.

By inserting an acupuncture needle or practicing moxibustion on a response point, one can recover the energetic balance of the body and treat, as well as prevent, disease. In fact, most "disease" begins with a blockage or imbalance of the body's energy.

When brain imaging techniques are applied to the study of acupuncture and moxibustion, the specifics of how this extraordinary process works will be more clearly revealed. I expect we will find that when moxibustion techniques are applied to the human body, they not only cause stimulation in the parts of the body to which they are directly applied, but they also stimulate the brain. I believe that acupuncture, acupressure, and moxibustion stimulate signals that are sent to the brain, telling it to begin repairing the body. Meridians, acupuncture points, and the body's own endocrine system are all part of this signaling process.

Again, when an appropriate stimulus is applied at a response point, it triggers the brain to engage the self-healing mechanism of the body. In this sense, it is more accurate to say that acupuncture and moxibustion do not heal the body; they stimulate the brain to heal the body.

In order to enjoy the healing benefits of acupuncture and moxibustion, we must overcome the resistance that we naturally experience when confronted with something unfamiliar. It is ironic and paradoxical that many humans can be brave in their pursuit of cosmetic changes such as body rings or tattoos, but can become anxious in the face of a needle or heated pulp, even if they are for the benefit of health!

By overcoming our fears and treating ourselves with acupuncture and moxibustion, we not only gain enhanced health but also experience the truth: my body is not me, but mine. We gain the power of self-control. In that sense, acupuncture, acupressure, and moxibustion are forms of self-discipline!

Performing Moxibustion

There are several methods of performing moxibustion—directly on to the skin, using a barrier, or in conjunction with acupuncture needles, to name a few.

Moxibustion can be categorized as either "direct" or "indirect." In both cases, an herb, usually dried mugwort, is burned on or near an acupressure point relating to a particular symptom.

With the indirect method, the flame does not make contact with the skin. The mugwort may be rolled into a densely packed cylinder, or a "moxa stick." The stick is then lit and held briefly a few millimeters above the acupressure point.

Moxibustion can also be used in conjunction with acupuncture needles, in which case a tuft of mugwort is put on the needle and burned.

You can purchase moxa sticks in Oriental medical clinics or Chinese herbal stores and use them very easily. Licensed acupuncturists usually practice moxibustion in conjunction with needles.

A third indirect method is to burn the mugwort with a barrier between the mugwort and the skin. The barrier can be any non-reactive material, even something organic, such as a thin slice of ginger, garlic, or salt, which may add natural medicinal benefits.

A fourth indirect method is lighting a larger piece of mugwort and then snuffing it out with a damp cloth or picking it off with tweezers when it gets too hot and the heat is close to the skin.

With direct moxibustion, the mugwort is burned on the surface of the skin. If allowed to burn out completely, the process may leave a small mark or blister. Although both methods are effective, direct moxibustion seems to bring the most immediate results.

The sensation of indirect moxibustion is much more subtle, delivering gentle warmth in the region to which it is applied. Direct moxibustion, on the other hand, delivers a more powerful surge of energy through the meridian channel, and therefore the effects are felt more readily. Additionally, direct moxibustion is very simple and economical, requiring only an inexpensive box of dried mugwort and some incense.

INDIRECT MOXIBUSTION WITH GINGER

1. Slice a 1/5-inch-thick piece of fresh ginger. Punch numerous holes in it and place it over a point.
2. Roll the mugwort or "moxa" into a cone shape approximately the size of a grapefruit seed or bigger.
3. Place this cone on top of the ginger slice.
4. Light it with incense and leave the moxa cone in place until it burns out.
5. Repeat this four more times on the same spot. As you repeat the procedure, you do not need to replace the ginger slice.

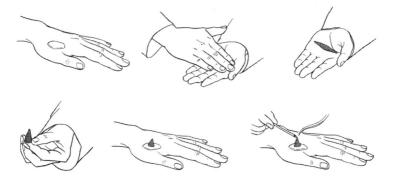

INDIRECT MOXIBUSTION WITH REMOVAL
1. Roll the moxa into a cone shape roughly the size of a grapefruit seed.
2. Place it on a healing point and light it with incense.
3. Wait until approximately 80 percent of the moxa cone burns, or until you feel intense heat. When it gets too hot, snuff it out with a damp cloth or remove the cone with tweezers or other tools and extinguish it in a bowl of water.

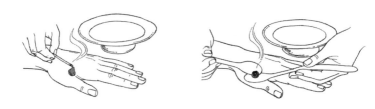

After practicing indirect moxibustion, a yellowish color might remain on your skin where you placed the moxa. This will disappear in a few days.

DIRECT MOXIBUSTION
1. Place the moxa between the left thumb and the index finger, and roll it gently into a cone shape.
2. With the right thumb and index finger, pull a piece of the rolled moxa—about half the size of a rice grain— off the top.
3. Moisten the surface of your left thumbnail with water or your saliva.
4. Place the moxa cone on top of your left thumbnail where you moistened it.
5. Now place the moxa cone on the desired healing point.

6. Light the moxa cone using a lit incense stick.
7. While the moxa cone is burning, apply gentle pressure around the area with your fingertips to distract from discomfort or pain.
8. Repeat this procedure four more times on the same healing point. Place the next moxa cone on top of the ashes of the previous one.

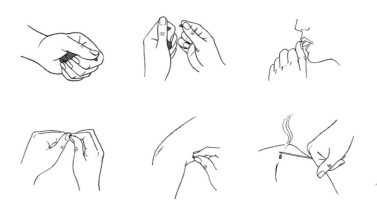

After the first two times, you may skip steps 3 and 4 (moistening the moxa cone before placing it on the point). After five repetitions, gently wipe away the ashes with a clean cloth. With direct moxibustion, a small scab might form after a day or two. Do not worry about this and continue to perform moxibustion on top of the scab.

Healing for Everyday Life

You can self-apply moxibustion to three key acupuncture points daily to maintain your overall health: Gok-ji, Jok-sam-lee, and Baek-hwe.

Each of the 365 acupuncture points is named poetically, originally with a Chinese character. The imagery of a point's name offers insight into either a point's benefits or location. For instance, the name Baek-hwe (Hundred Convergences) literally means, "intersecting point of one hundred meridians." The Jok-sam-lee (Leg Three Mile) point earned its name because it gives a person an extra three miles of energy.

In addition to its name, each point is assigned an identification number to track its placement along the body. Point location numbers, such as LU11 or ST36, are a standard referencing system used by professional acupuncturists, and so I use them as an additional label. You do not need to know or remember any of these numbers to practice the self-moxibustion and acupressure techniques in this book.

Gok-ji (Pool at the Bend, LI2)

Location: Place your palm on the middle of your chest and find the creases on the elbow. The point is located at the end of the crease on your arm. Find the corresponding point on the other arm as well. [Fig.1]

Effective for: strengthening the large and small intestines, migraines, numbness in shoulders or arms, skin conditions, and reproductive diseases.

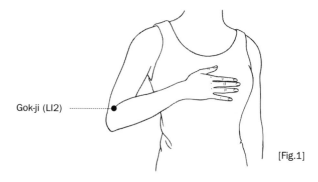

Gok-ji (LI2) ·············●

[Fig.1]

Jok-sam-lee (Leg Three Mile, ST36)

Location: Place the pads of four fingers under the knee cap. The point is located below the fingers and in between the slight depression formed by the bones. Find the corresponding point on the other leg. [Fig.2]

Effective for: lowering high blood pressure, strengthening weak limbs, preventing dizziness, and aiding recovery from stroke.

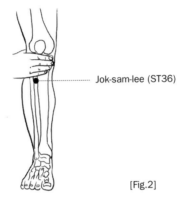

Jok-sam-lee (ST36)

[Fig.2]

Baek-hwe (Hundred Convergences, GV20)

Location: From both ear holes, draw two imaginary lines up to the top of the head until they meet from the highest points

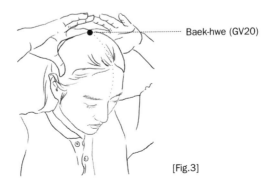

Baek-hwe (GV20)

[Fig.3]

on the ears. Then, draw one line from the tip of the nose straight up to the top of the head. The Baek-hwe is located where the three lines intersect on top of the head. [Fig.3]

Effective for: headaches, weakness from stroke, poor memory, hemorrhoids, and poor hearing.

Moxibustion for Common Symptoms

Common Cold or Flu

Do moxibustion on these three points for ten consecutive days to treat a cold or the flu. Since they are located on your back, you will need to ask someone else to do the moxibustion for you.

Dae-chu (Great Hammer, GV14): Right below the 7th cervical vertebrae. You can locate this point by bending your head forward and finding the biggest bone where the neck and the shoulders meet. Place your finger right below this bone. Now return your head to an upright position. Make sure you find the point to do moxibustion after the head has returned;

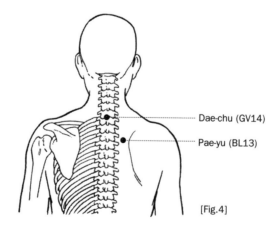

Dae-chu (GV14)

Pae-yu (BL13)

[Fig.4]

when the head returns to an upright position, the location rises slightly. [Fig.4]

Pae-yu (Lung Shu, BL13): Find the groove between the 3rd and 4th thoracic vertebrae—approximately at the crest of the shoulder blades. The Pae-yu point is located halfway between the groove on the spine and the crest of the shoulder blade. Find the corresponding point on the other side of the body as well. Perform moxibustion on both sides. [Fig.4]

Yeol-kuel (Broken Sequence, LU7): Cross your index fingers and the thumbs of both hands with the index finger of the other. The point is located in the depression right under the tip of the index finger, next to the bone and toward the inside. [Fig.5]

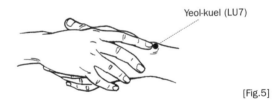

Yeol-kuel (LU7)

[Fig.5]

STOMACH AND DIGESTIVE PROBLEMS

Hap-kok (Union Valley, LI4): The end of the crease that forms between your thumb and the index fingers when you put them together. *This point is contraindicated for pregnant women.* [Fig.6]

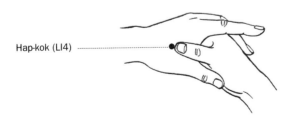

Hap-kok (LI4)

[Fig.6]

Jok-sam-lee (Leg Three Mile, ST36): Place the pads of four fingers under the kneecap. The point is located below the fingers and in between the slight depression formed by the bones. Find the corresponding point on the other leg. [Fig.2]

Gok-ji (Pool at the Bend, LI11): Put your palm on the middle of the chest and find the creases on the elbow. The point is located at the end of the crease on your arm. Find the corresponding point on the other arm as well. [Fig.1]

Sam-eum-gyo (Three Yin Intersection, SP6): Place the pads of four fingers on the anklebone (the bone that sticks out on the inner side of the ankle) at the depression just under the shin bone. *This point is contraindicated for pregnant women.* [Fig.7]

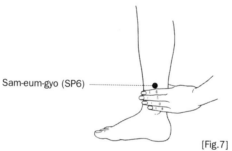

Sam-eum-gyo (SP6)

[Fig.7]

Lower Back Pain

Hu-gye (Back Ravine, SI3): When you make a loose fist, the point is located at the end of the crease, the highest point and the junction of the red and white skin [Fig.8]

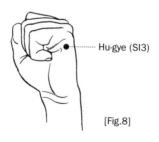

Hu-gye (SI3)

[Fig.8]

Yong-chun (Gushing Spring, KI1): Divide the main body of the foot into 3 equal parts. Yong-chun is one third the distance from the top of the toes, at the center of the sole.[Fig.9]

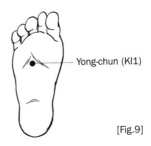

Yong-chun (KI1)

[Fig.9]

Facial Puffiness

Yin-reung-chun (Yin Mound Spring, SP9): Below the inner knee and the depression along the shin bone (tibia). Those who often wake up with a puffy face can practice moxibustion or acupressure on this point to make the puffiness disappear. *This point is contraindicated for pregnant women.* [Fig.10]

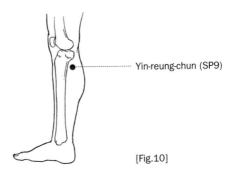

Yin-reung-chun (SP9)

[Fig.10]

Wrist, Arm, or Shoulder Pain

Yang-ji (Yang Pool, TH4): Raise your hand upward to find the crease on your wrist. The point is located at the depression formed in the middle of the crease. [Fig.11]

EAR INFECTIONS, RINGING IN THE EARS

Jung-jeu (Central Islet, TH3): Directly behind the 4th and 5th metacarpal bones or knuckles. [Fig.11]

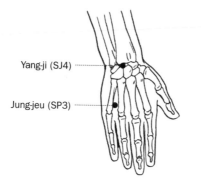

Yang-ji (SJ4)

Jung-jeu (SP3)

[Fig.11]

KNEE PAIN

Dok-bi (Calf's Nose, ST35): Below the kneecap. They are the two depressions you find under the knee. [Fig.12]

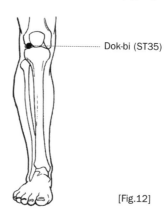

Dok-bi (ST35)

[Fig.12]

HEADACHES

Baek-hwe (Hundred Convergences, GV20): Draw two imaginary lines up to the top of the head until they meet from the highest points on the ears. Then, draw one line from the tip of the nose straight up to the top of the head. The Baek-hwe is located where the three lines intersect on top of the head. [Fig.3]

Acupressure for Self-Healing

During my childhood, most houses had a set of acupuncture needles as a first aid kit of sorts. When I had severe indigestion, my grandfather would take a needle and prick the very tip of my thumb, letting a drop of blood flow. This stimulation and release of a single drop of blood would open the blockages in my meridian channels. He would then rub my back with his warm hands. Then to my amazement, the food that had been stuck somewhere between my mouth and my stomach would gently settle down, making me feel much better.

It is truly regrettable that acupuncture techniques used in Asia over a long history as daily remedies have now become distant to the general public. Since in many regions the law limits practicing acupuncture even among family members, I will introduce the techniques of acupressure as an alternative.

Acupressure and acupuncture are basically alike. Both of them use the same points. While acupuncturists apply needles, practitioners of acupressure use the fingers or pointy instruments to press key points on the surface of the skin that stimulate the body's self-healing abilities.

In the United States acupressure is primarily used to relieve pain, reduce stress, and improve overall well-being. In Asia, the technique is used more like first aid: individuals typically practice it on themselves or on family members to treat everyday ailments such as colds, headaches, sore muscles, and hangovers. While many people prefer to go to a trained therapist to get acupressure treatments, the techniques, once learned, can be self-administered or administered by a family member.

Foremost among the advantages of acupressure is that it is safe to perform on yourself and others—even if you have never done it before—so long as you follow the instructions and pay attention to the warnings. You need only your hands to practice acupressure therapy anytime, anywhere.

Tension tends to concentrate around acupressure points. When a muscle is chronically tense or in spasm, the muscle fibers contract due to the secretion of lactic acid caused by fatigue, trauma, stress, chemical imbalances, or poor circulation.

As a point is pressed, the muscle tension yields to the pressure of the fingers, enabling the fibers to elongate and relax, blood to flow freely, and toxins to be released. Increased circulation also brings more oxygen and other nutrients to affected areas, which increases the body's resistance to illness and promotes a healthier, more vital life.

When you apply acupressure to certain points, use your thumbs, fingers, palms, or the side of your hand to apply steady, stationary pressure for three to five seconds on the acupuncture points. Repeat this firm pressure for three to five times.

Never press on an open wound, swollen or inflamed skin, a bruise, surgery scar, varicose veins, or broken bones. Avoid acupressure if you have a contagious disease, an infectious skin disease, or a serious heart, kidney, or lung disorder. Avoid acupressure in the area of a known tumor. Certain acupressure points must be avoided during pregnancy.

By using a combination of HT self-care methods including meridian exercises, deep abdominal breathing, meditation, and moxibustion, you can improve your condition as well as feel more alive, serene, and healthy.

Acupressure for Common Symptoms

COMMON COLD OR FLU

Poong-mun (Wind Gate, BL12): Two finger widths on either side of the second thoracic vertebrae. This is the most vulnerable point where cold and damp energy may initially enter the body. [Fig.13]

Dae-chu (Great Hammer, GV14): Right below the 7th cervical vertebrae. You can locate this point by bending your head forward and finding the biggest bone where the neck and the shoulders meet. Place your finger right below this bone. Now return your head to an upright position. Make sure you find the point after the head has returned; when the head returns to an upright position, the location moves up slightly. [Fig.13]

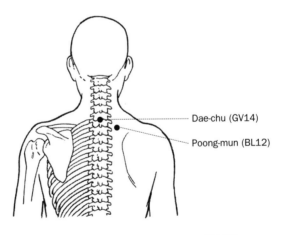

Dae-chu (GV14)

Poong-mun (BL12)

[Fig.13]

Joong-bu (Central Treasury, LU1): Place your middle fingers in the hollow areas directly below the protrusions of the collarbone just outside your upper breastbone. Press this point with your thumb or make a fist with your right hand with your thumb folded in and gently tap this point on the left side. Do this for one to three minutes and then switch sides. If this is too painful or if blockages still remain, rub the pressure points with the pads of your fingers. [Fig.14]

Oon-mun (Cloud Gate, LU2): Just below the collarbone on either side of your shoulders. Press this point with your thumb or make a fist with your right hand with your thumb folded in and gently tap this point on the left side. Do this for one to three minutes and then switch sides. If this is too painful or if blockages still remain, rub the pressure points with the pads of your fingers. [Fig.14]

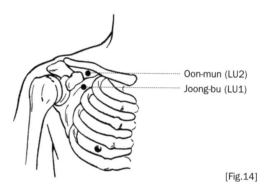

Oon-mun (LU2)
Joong-bu (LU1)

[Fig.14]

Stomachaches

Hap-kok (Union Valley, LI4): At the end of the crease that forms between your thumb and the index fingers when you put them together. Having someone else press down on these points on both hands simultaneously is most effective. It might be a little painful, but try to bear it. Press down for a slow count of five and release for a count of five as well. Repeat several times. [Fig.6]

Tae-chung (Great Surge, LV3): Between the big toe and the second toe, one-half inch in from where they form a web.

Press down on the points on both feet at the same time. This is good for easing stomachaches caused by indigestion.

Rub the stomach and the back: Lie down and have someone rub your stomach or back with a comforting circular motion. Make sure you keep both areas covered and unexposed to cold air. This helps food settle into your stomach and eases digestion. [Fig.15]

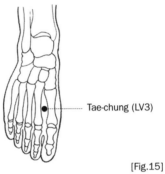

Tae-chung (LV3)

[Fig.15]

HEADACHES

Poong-ji (Wind Pool, GB 20): Two inches out from the middle of your neck, underneath the base of the skull. Use the thumbs of both hands to press these points. Sit on a chair and bend over, with your elbows propped on a table or desk, to make the sustained pressure on these points most comfortable. [Fig.16]

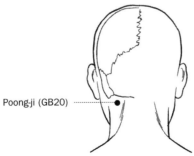

Poong-ji (GB20)

[Fig.16]

Tae-yang: The area of the temples. By using the thumbs, press this point for three to five seconds. Repeat this slowly five times. Then tap this point lightly thirty times using the fingertips. [Fig.17]

Gak-son (Angle Vertex, TH20): Directly above the apex of the ear on your hairline. [Fig.17]

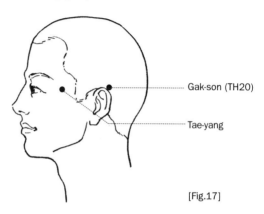

Gak-son (TH20)

Tae-yang

[Fig.17]

Yeol-kuel (Broken Sequence, LU7): Cross your index fingers and the thumbs of both hands with the index finger of the other hand. The point is located in the depression right under the tip of the index finger, next to the bone and toward the inside. [Fig.5]

Boost Your Immune System

Joong-bu (Central Treasury, LU1): Place your middle fingers in the hollow area directly below the protrusions of the collarbone just outside your upper breastbone. Breathe deeply as you press this point with your thumb for one minute. [Fig.14]

Jok-sam-lee (Leg Three Mile, ST36): Place the pads of four fingers under the kneecap. The point is located below the fingers and in between the slight depression formed by the bones. Find the corresponding point on the other leg. [Fig.2]

Small Repairs

Most of us have a hammer, nails, and other tools for making basic repairs in our homes, as well as the ability to use them. If we make small repairs as they occur, our house remains well maintained and will last a long time. However, if we leave them unfixed, ultimately, the damage to the structure becomes so overwhelming that big renovations are necessary. The same principle applies to the human body.

Acupuncture, acupressure, and moxibustion are like the hammer and nails we use to repair and maintain our houses. Anyone who has the ability to use a hammer and nails can practice acupuncture, acupressure, and moxibustion. You do not need the skills of an architect or builder to use a nail and hammer in the maintenance of your house. In much the same way, you do not need to know about all the structures and functions of the human body to use acupuncture, acupressure, and moxibustion. Moreover, we possess an amazing functional control panel called the brain. If we take the simplest measures to activate its functions, the brain will automatically take care of the rest.

It is a sign of maturity to have the ability to manage our bodies and maintain our health as well as our family's well-being. Perhaps this should be a requirement before creating families!

6

Human Technology and Sexuality

I HAVE GIVEN INNUMERABLE LECTURES while traveling around the world during the past twenty-five years. I had many opportunities to have conversation with people of diverse social, cultural, and religious backgrounds about the way of life. During this process, I came upon an important discovery. The attitude and experience of sexuality have vastly influenced the quality of life in both positive and negative ways.

Most people think they have a mature perspective and comfortable relationship with sex. The reality is different. I have found that too many people have twisted or dual perspectives on sex. This reality often prevents people from leading more fulfilling and authentic lives. The times I feel most saddened is when I meet people who have had sexual traumas and suffer from it for the rest of their lives.

For this reason, I have emphasized that sex education must take place at home before our children reach puberty and before they are too much exposed to immature social notions of sex. I include sex education in the family as an important part of Human Technology. Before talking about sex education, allow me to share some general HT perspective on sex in this chapter.

The Brain Loves Sex

Sexuality is one of the most powerful energies we will ever experience. Sex can be described as passionate and animalistic, or as majestic, exalted, and sacred. For some, these perspectives may be "bookends" for the range of possible interpretations of sexuality. Yet even these views are too limited. Human Technology embraces sexuality as central to life, and intends to expand our experience, understanding, and application of this magnificent energy. As we relate more to sex as an experience of our spirit and not just of the senses, our expression of sexual energy in our lives can shift dramatically.

From a biological point of view, our capacity to desire sex—and to experience pleasure from it—is natural and deeply hard-wired in our brains. Millions of years of evolution have given us a wonderfully sophisticated system of brain pathways and hormonal regulators that make us feel good and spur our rituals of attraction and union.

Neurologists say that even the emotion called love, strictly speaking, arises for the most part out of the activity of the brain. This is because the emotions that arouse love are caused by the actions of chemical substances secreted by the cerebrum. They say sexual desires are associated with the body's chemistry such as dopamine and noradrenalin. It is the brain that loves sex.

Your experience of sex is both private and important to your well-being. I hope you will create conditions that align your sexuality with your health, your well-being, and your life purpose. I hope you will realize your power of choice, release guilt, and be aware of sexual responsibilities.

HT Guidelines on Sexuality

We each have the right to choose how we feel about and experience sex. Although cultural groups have laws about sexual practices, many of them controversial and subject to debate, sexual decisions should remain in the hands of the individual.

There are many outdated notions about sex that make us feel needlessly guilty. In human history, a sense of shame and guilt about sex has somehow been implanted in our minds, whether we are aware of it or not. Overly moralizing standards have bound human concepts so that they have acted as significant impediments to the well-being of individuals. Astonishingly, there are still places in our society where sexual doctrines dictate lethal punishment for some expressions of sexuality.

Let's get rid of our guilt about sex. Our nature is simply our nature, and there is no benefit in getting wrapped up in debates about "lower" or "higher." All life begins with sex. Without sexual intercourse, none of us would be here. Depending on our value system and our attitudes, sex, a natural phenomenon, can make us smile blissfully, put a spring in our step, and make us happy.

Of course I am not advocating licentiousness or carelessness.

We must be aware of our sexual responsibilities. We may encounter situations where sexual feelings are not reciprocated, or have no outlet. We need maturity, wisdom, and skills to handle such circumstances.

According to our values and choices, sex can be an act of love or debasement. Mature sex is an art, a healing, true communication that unites the body and spirit. A powerful drive, sex has the potential to exert inappropriate influence over our judgment. Sex can be used to cause harm, as a means of controlling others or inflating the ego; it can become an absorbing habit—even an addiction—that leads to a disconnection from the rich texture of human relationships or our spirituality.

But allow me to make a different point as well, about the meaning of "responsibility." Often, when people hear this word, they think about their worst deed or the biggest mistake they have ever made. "Being responsible" means guilty acceptance of the consequences or punishment. This meaning of responsibility is often not helpful and may be harmful.

The true meaning of responsibility lies in accepting that you are the creator. It means understanding and accepting that you create your circumstances and your experience: "This is my life and I created this." Responsibility does not mean passive acceptance or resignation, but dignity and authority.

Thus, your experience of sexuality is ultimately your own creation. Please create your sexual life consciously, in the image of your own grandest vision, to reflect your truest values and desires!

An Energetic View of Sex

I have devoted a great deal of my life to sharing energy sensitivity training methods, and have developed mind-body connection programs that are intended to heighten our powers of perception and enrich and broaden our experience of life on earth.

Sex is called Seong in Korean. The character Seong combines

two characters: one means "mind," and the other means "to be born" or "to come into being." Thus, sex means "the place where the mind comes into being." Here "mind" refers to the Universal Mind, the fundamental source of all creation. This interpretation reflects that sexual energy is regarded as an important and powerful force in our lives.

There is a difference between sexual energy and the life-energy that circulates through Su-seung-hwa-gang (see Chapter 3). Sexual energy is a special form of this life-energy. When sexual energy in the lower abdomen area (Dahn-jon) is activated, it doesn't stay there quietly, but moves. It has a tendency to "wander" around the body if not managed well, and can "rise" to the head, manifesting in preoccupations or dreams.

We can use Dahn-jon breathing (see Chapter 4) to concentrate and transform our sexual energy. Through diligent and consistent practice of Dahn-jon breathing, Su-seung-hwa-gang circulation improves and Dahn-jon energy increases. *A strong Dahn-jon acts as a magnet for scattered sexual energy.* The weaker the Dahn-jon, the more vulnerable one is to being controlled by sexual desires. It is a good idea to build basic physical strength, get balanced, and practice Dahn-jon breathing to accumulate and transform your sexual energy.

Furthermore, depending on your attention and choice, you may use this energy to enhance and deepen your sexual experience. Energy can be focused on any of your three main energy centers or Dahn-jons, upper (forehead), middle (chest), and lower (abdomen) helping you to embrace the spiritual, emotional, and physical aspects of sexuality.

In a similar way, concentrated sexual energy can be used to heighten your overall vitality and passion for life. It can power the creation of art, writing, music, or even social or political endeavors. When sexual energy flows naturally, we experience the greatest harmony in our human relationships.

I hope that these HT guidelines and exercises will inspire you to create a vital, positive place for sexuality in your life, as is your right.

7

Talking to Children about Sexuality

HAVE YOU EVER SHARED A CONVERSATION with your children about sex? For many parents, when children reach a certain age it becomes difficult to discuss sexual issues with them.

Sometimes during seminars, I ask the parents in the audience if they have discussed sex with their children. If they say no, I ask "So, if you do not have a conversation about sex with your child, would you want your next-door neighbor to do it for you?" This usually gets their attention and elicits chuckles while highlighting the absurd paradox that characterizes much of our experience of sex education.

Whose responsibility is it to educate our children about sexuality? I hope you share my sense of absurdity about asking this question. I consider the sexual education of children to be one of the most critical tasks of parenting. Given the power of sexual energy, why would we give away the authority to teach our children about sexuality?

Befriending the Body

Many couples cannot communicate honestly about sex, so it is not surprising that this topic is difficult to communicate to children. For children and adults alike, the first step to being comfortable with discussions about sexuality is being comfortable with our bodies.

Children should be comfortable with every aspect of their bodies from as early an age as possible. Once they are old enough to be curious about human anatomy, we should teach them the names and functions of all our organs.

The health tools we described in Chapter 5 have the added benefit of helping us gain this familiarity. Acupressure and moxibustion allow us to be intimate with ourselves and others we trust in a safe, healing environment. Such practice can easily lead to natural, comfortable discussions about sexual anatomy or sexual energy. When we address sexuality from a healing perspective, our children will be more likely to think of sex in terms of love, trust, and mutual respect.

Talking about Sex

In a way appropriate to the child's comprehension level, parents should talk early and frequently, before puberty, about the power of sexual energy. Talk to them about how it is possible to unexpectedly encounter sexual feelings for different people and how this ebb and flow is natural to the rhythm of life. We have a reservoir of life experience from which to draw, and we can talk about the many faces of sexual energy.

Most of us can look back and think of examples of experiencing "puppy love" and innocent infatuations. We can distinguish when sexual energy took the form of lust, passion, or transformed creativity. If we have the experience of a long-term committed relationship or marriage, then we can describe how sexual energy can deepen our bonds over the course of our lives.

We should also discuss the purpose and possible outcomes of sex. They should be aware that sexual activity can be any or all of the following: the means of creating life, an activity of physical pleasure, and a form of emotional and spiritual connection. They should also realize that sex can result in unwanted pregnancies and infectious diseases.

Unfortunately, in this era we also have the burden of explaining how sexuality has become commercialized through the mass media. Children must understand that our culture is now saturated with images of sexuality that are mostly intended to direct consumer behavior. Although it is not possible to protect children from every negative influence, we must do our best to minimize their exposure.

There can be no absolute rule for at what age it is appropriate to have sex. Cultural norms differ, and individuals vary according to their level of physical, mental and emotional maturity. In any case, having sex without a clear understanding of its physiological consequences, or doing so in the absence of trust and mutual respect, can hardly be viewed as beneficial.

I suggest that while both parents should talk with their children about sexuality, fathers should be the primary teachers for their daughters and mothers for their sons. This recommendation may seem counterintuitive, but it offers the potential for much deeper teaching if the parent is highly aware and enlightened about their sexuality.

When the parent of opposite gender explains sexuality, the child is more likely to understand sex as an energetic exchange, rather than simply an urge to be managed. Also, given the difficult sexual histories of so many adults, I believe it is easier for a father to offer wise, compassionate, non-judgmental guidance to his daughter, and a mother to offer it to her son.

Although these topics are useful conceptually, please remember that, as always, we must connect theory and action. Dialogue alone is not a panacea for a culture with dysfunctional sexual ideas and behaviors. Because of entrenched cultural mores, our sexual beliefs and habits tend to be relatively resistant to change. Improved conceptual understanding of sexuality does not guarantee enlightened sexual behavior as the child grows older.

Being a role model of enlightened sexuality is thus all the more critical for our children's learning. In sexuality, as with all life experience, we must be the change we wish to see in the world.

Through these discussions, we will be able to develop a basis of trust with our children, leading to better communication. When we can speak about sex with our children, we will find that it frees our ability to talk about other topics. These conversations will assure our children that they are being respected, which will lead them to develop self-worth, responsibility, and maturity. Through these sincere, honest discussions, you may even change your own preconceptions.

Exercising Wisdom

Think back to what you consider was the worst choice in your life. If you could go back in time and get a chance to relive that moment, knowing what you know now, would you choose differently? Probably. If someone you respected had told you about encountering a similar situation when they were young, you may well not have gone "down that road" in the first place. Such storytelling can be invaluable, giving your children a sense of anticipation about possible life paths, thereby creating more confidence for them to make their own choices.

Sexuality is far from the only critical issue that requires parental guidance. It is no less vital to teach our children about responsibility and dignity, caring and concern, acceptance of differences, courage in the face of adversity, and doing what we say—all the values that make life worthwhile, harmonious and fun.

The more consistent we are in engaging our children in such dialogues, the richer and more meaningful our lives will become. If we maintain open communication with our children, sexuality will become simply another natural, dynamic topic that increases our appreciation for one another and life itself.

8

Journey to the Soul: Reflection

HUMAN TECHNOLOGY (HT) HELPS people gain and use practical tools for life. But tools have value only if they are used meaningfully. Thus, it is fitting that HT include an exploration of the purpose of life. It is not my intention to offer the following three chapters as religious doctrine.

These teachings are based on my direct personal experience, and I suspect that most sensible persons would agree with these simple ideas. I believe we all have a gut sense that it is possible to hear the voice of the soul. There is no proof. I can only tell you that I feel my soul, and I cherish it as my true essence.

So please read the next three chapters as a guide to the soul's journey, in nonreligious language, for a 21st century human. We can describe this path in three successive stages: reflection, awakening, and choice and being.

"Who am I?" "What is the purpose of my life?" These questions arise spontaneously throughout our lives, either unbidden or through conscious intent. Anyone who wishes to live an authentic life must answer these questions, regardless of whether they believe in the existence of the soul or practice a religion. If these queries remain unanswered, life will more than likely remain superficial and empty, in spite of any material abundance. If you wish to make the soul's journey, then I suggest you ask yourself these questions relentlessly and ruthlessly, and listen carefully.

Voice of the Soul

There are many types of sounds within us, such as those of our bodies, thoughts, and emotions. If we are attentive, we may notice that something or someone is constantly speaking. When we remain silent and listen intently as others speak to us, we are not hearing an outside voice only. Something is continually speaking within us. That being constantly reacts to all the information that we see and hear. In fact, that being is reacting even as you read this.

Our experience and knowledge is constantly being edited as we think, "I feel cold." "I feel hot." "I am hungry." "That person is attractive." On some occasions, when our mind is at peace, we can hear a different, distinctive voice.

As usual, another day is passing. The weather is beautiful. I am taking a break from work to look outside my window. My body feels at ease, and my mind is clear and tranquil. From the depths of my heart, I feel a certain sense of yearning, a sense of loss, as if I have lost something very important. I cannot explain the feeling.

Then I suddenly hear, "Can this be it?" "What am I doing

right now?" I look around me, as I am surprised to hear these kinds of questions. I feel self-conscious and awkward, so I hastily return to my work. Throughout the day, I keep recalling that unfamiliar voice. However, I do not tell anyone about it. I keep it concealed in my heart. That voice becomes masked by the noises of the world, and I forget about it for a long time.

If you have had this kind of experience before, try to recall it and how you felt in that moment. Whose voice do you think it was? I believe it was the voice of your soul.

I am confident that you have heard similar voices and pondered such questions at some point in your life. But the so-called "adult responsibilities" of day-to-day living distract our focus from these larger questions of life. Our priorities become heavily, even completely, tilted towards our immediate sensory needs. We become preoccupied with how to survive, rather than why. We may even forget that we ever asked such questions.

That is a tragic point in human experience, because that is the point at which life can become meaningless. We try to supply meaning by asserting that our lives are about our families, our loved ones, our jobs or our religion. But at the deepest place of our being, as important as these things certainly are, we sense that *there must be something more.* There must be some *reason* for it all, some *purpose* behind it all. There has to be something more than just day-to-day survival.

And so the questions are buried deep within our heart, remaining hidden and often forgotten during our lifetime, until it is time to depart this world. Suddenly the questions become important again. At that moment we may realize that we have lived without ever knowing ourselves, or why we have even lived at all. When it is time to go, we may feel bewildered…*What was this all about? What was the point of it all?*

Taking a Journey

We often compare life to a journey, but more often than not, it is closer to a wandering. This is because for many, the destination is not clear. A wanderer does not know where to go, while a person on a journey has a specific destination in mind.

When we have a clear idea of who we are and why we live, our lives become a journey. A story is created about our lives. And when the end comes, even if the story adds up to only one line, the story reaches a settled conclusion.

> *Like many others, I also heard that voice one day. I was not necessarily attentive to that voice from the beginning. However, I began to like it as time passed. I grew closer to that voice, and we started to share many things. I shared my sadness, joy, sense of defeat and victory, my pleasure and pain. Ultimately, we shared peace and a smile.*
>
> *I discovered something long after I became friends with that voice. I realized it never ceased to speak, regardless of whether I paid attention to it. That voice had been talking to me not only while I was awake, but also while I was asleep. I simply had not heard the voice due to other noises drowning it out. Sounds of the body, thoughts, and emotions are usually louder and rowdier than the voice of the soul. They tend to speak more, causing the voice of the soul to get lost easily.*

We can only begin to hear the soul's voice after the sounds of our bodies, thoughts, and emotions become softer. Before the soul begins its journey, these sounds, thoughts, and emotions fundamentally concern the body. Our bodies may have specific desires in different situations, but we generally long for security, recognition, and control. We try to feel secure by possessing material things. We tend to be satisfied when others give us recognition. We have a sense of superiority and confidence when we feel in control of situations or people around us.

If these three desires are not satisfied, our bodies, thoughts, and emotions continue to make noise: "Do not even think about taking that away from me!" "How dare you disregard me?" "Listen to me and do as I say!"

The voice of the soul, on the other hand, has no interest in such egotism. For example, if we try very hard to become famous and succeed, we may hear that voice saying, "Now are you satisfied? Is this truly what you want?"

In order to hear the voice of our soul, we must be able to quiet the sounds of the body, our thoughts, and our emotions.

HT breathing techniques, meditation, and meridian exercises benefit not only our health or energy levels, but can also bring us to states of deep calm, where we can more easily hear the soul.

"Who am I? Why am I here?" How will the soul answer these questions? In the beginning you may hear, "I am this person, who does this job." Of course, these are perfectly reasonable answers, and they may be exactly what you need to hear at a given time.

But I challenge you to keep asking these questions, until you no longer receive literal or conceptual answers. If we approach these questions with deep effort and sincerity, they can penetrate straight through the masks of job, personality, ethnicity, gender, or any other ego reference. Eventually we awaken to the realization that these two questions are one and the same, and the answer to one solves the other. That answer goes beyond words, and it is likely to reorder your life priorities on the grandest of scales.

9

Journey of the Soul: Awakening

WHEN YOU REFLECT ON YOUR LIFE, you may feel unhappy. A life crisis may precipitate even more acute questioning. We may feel overwhelmed to the point of emptiness. Please embrace the discontent and emptiness. Do not avoid these feelings by seeking distractions, for they may be the beginning of your awakening.

What are the principles that can sustain our awakening? How can we understand the world, after we have decided to listen to the soul's voice and follow its call?

Suffering

Life as a physical body is suffering. There are times, of course, when life is beautiful and even uplifting. However, when we examine life in its whole picture, it is filled with unwanted happenings and hardships.

The fact that we were born to live in this world out of an external force and not our own choosing is in itself suffering. We live trapped inside time, space, and the limitations of our physical bodies, embracing the loneliness of the soul.

"Happiness is a state of mind." "Choose to be happy." "Create your own happiness." Why do we need so many self-motivational maxims? After spending your whole day in the never-ending pursuit of happiness, have you ever gone to bed wishing that tomorrow would not come again, overwhelmed by the heaviness of life?

If life is a source of continuous happiness, then we may not need philosophy or spirituality. We do not normally bother ourselves with the meaning of life when we feel happy. When happiness recedes, we question the meaning of life. "Why is this happening to me?" "What point is there to life?" When happiness returns, we forget about these questions. But then another change arrives and we question again. "How can this happen to me again?"

The conditions that make us content do not last forever. Eventually, they are bound to disappear, and we will once again find ourselves wondering about the meaning of life. Only when we mature sufficiently to the point where we are no longer deceived by this repetitive cycle, do we begin to question ourselves deeply and earnestly.

Eventually we strip off the layers of meaning that we had so carefully constructed around our lives, a process that leads to emptiness and loneliness. Most of us cannot bear this loneliness. We try our best to forget these questions, yet we remain haunted always by their echoes in the back of our minds. However, if we wish to realize the truth behind life, we need the courage to look this emptiness straight in the eye.

When you have realized that life is basically suffering punctuated by fleeting moments of happiness, when you accept that state of unbearable emptiness, then you will know you are on the path of the soul. When you find yourself demanding the unchanging truth with all your being, know that voice and remember it. You need courage and discipline to hold on to these questions that cry out from the depth of your soul.

Transience

The second teaching to realize is transience. Transience is the most general phenomenon of the cosmos. Change is the only changeless reality. Seasons, livelihoods, personal relationships—all of these will change.

Our experiences in life are transient and relative. Only death is certain, completing the cycle of life that begins with birth. By meditating upon this truth, we recognize that we, too, are manifestations of transience.

When we understand this teaching deeply, we become humble and sincere. We treasure each moment and endeavor to do our best. We feel less stress and become more accepting of the diverse phenomena of life. If something "good" happens we can feel the joy and be thankful. But we know that the conditions for the situation will not last forever, and we do not become attached to the feeling. We will simply consider every moment and every experience as a blessing.

Moreover, we come to feel deep compassion and love for those around us who have not awakened to this truth. They seem as children, and we love them as tenderly. To live this realization requires great courage and endurance. The prospect of death at any moment brings no fear. In the moment that we realize transience, we are awake to the desire to know our true essence.

In today's world of accelerating change, I think most readers are already conceptually familiar with transience. Rather, the challenge has more to do with our brains and bodies. It is our brains and bodies that become easily conditioned to fixed expectations.

Our task is to adapt our *physiology* to the realization of transience. We may not like the feeling of emptiness that accompanies constant change, or we may be attached to particular circumstances that make for contentedness. Those feelings and attachments have a physical basis in the nervous system, and physical training can help us gain control over the associated chemistry and neural wiring. Brain Respiration, especially BR Versatilizing (see Chapter 12), is ideally suited for helping us to appreciate transience as a bodily reality, and making it a life habit.

No-Self

Beyond transience, there is still a deeply rooted pretense that remains. We may accept that the outside world is transitory and variable, but still we take refuge in the reality of the self itself. Descartes, for example, famously doubted all phenomena except his own existence.

But here is the final truth. Even "I" is a delusion. In fact, it is our delusion of "I" that generates our original ignorance of transience. For clinging to "I" is the first attachment. It is only through "I" that transience can cause pain. If "I" is real and stable, then "I" wishes for its surroundings to endure as well. All attachment and pain are born of our belief in the reality of "I."

Effective training to realize Mu-ah (literally "no-self" in Korean) is the most difficult of all. In past times, spiritual masters put their students through all manner of grievous hardship so they could awaken to egolessness. Such methods can be profoundly effective but there is no guarantee. I myself underwent twenty-one days of fasting and sleep deprivation, but I do not recommend this to anyone. Nonetheless, if you do wish to train to achieve Mu-ah, then I suggest you begin with meditation. Let yourself be guided to a teacher who is right for you.

Life events may be the best training of all. Your reaction to a thoughtless remark, a call for help, or your actions can all be used. Through a simple but radical shift in perspective, you will find that your life is full of opportunities to experience Mu-ah.

Keep in mind that realizing Mu-ah does not require a position of "meek selflessness." Mu-ah is available in any moment, whether mundane or climactic. In fact, the deepest experiences of Mu-ah may be imperceptible or counterintuitive to an insensitive observer. Washing a dish, being one with the setting sun, even training for a battle—all of these may be authentic realizations of Mu-ah.

Finally, let me share with you the most compelling reason to be Mu-ah. *It is through Mu-ah that the greatest creativity is manifest.* "I" always has some degree of smallness motivating its creative actions. By its very definition and nature, "I" is a contraction to a single, limited perspective.

Allow me ask you a question. Has your knowledge delivered you the answers to the most important questions of life? Has your experience delivered you the answers to the most important questions of life?

When you are trapped inside the "I" that you know, the "I" that you have experienced, you cannot use your true creativity. Knowledge and experience are not who you are. They are simply the "I" that you know and experience. Someone who will only take the road that they see an end to, a road that has already been tested, is not a creative person. A great soul creates a road if one cannot be seen.

True creation is only possible when you step outside all your previous experiences, when you step outside the "I" that you have experienced. When you are trapped inside the "I" that you have experienced, you ceaselessly doubt your ability to create. When we encounter Mu-ah, all limits created by the "I" formed by your experiences vanish and infinite creativity springs forth. It is when we become Mu-ah that transience and emptiness become the basis for true creation. When we realize Mu-ah, we shed the boundaries of the individual in favor of infinite potential. To be Mu-ah is to connect with the Creator.

Being Mu-ah means that you are showing the world a potential of your brain that you have never experienced before. At this moment, you are born anew to an "I" that you have never experienced before. When we become Mu-ah we stand below Heaven, atop the earth, and realize our full potential as great souls that can ceaselessly create.

I hope these teachings will be valuable for your soul's journey. Awakening to suffering, transience and Mu-ah are timeless principles that cannot be avoided if one is traveling the soul's path. As you realize these truths, you will then have the power and responsibility of choice at the highest level.

10

Journey with the Soul:
Choice and Being

IF WE HAVE EXPERIENCED OUR SOUL'S AWAKENING, then we now have several options. One may choose to live as the voice directs. It is also possible to doubt the voice or come up with an excuse to avoid it. The most common scenario is fluctuating between two alternatives: at times feeling empowered in our passionate fulfillment of soul purpose and at other times reverting to old habits.

Following the path of the soul's purpose can be rewarding and joyful, and it can be overwhelmingly difficult. At challenging junctures, we must choose again whether or not to continue on the path. During this process, our soul is an indispensable guide. Our soul knows when we are faithful or not. If we listen closely to the voice of our soul, it will show us the way. It tells us exactly how to prevail when obstacles block us. Whether we heed, or even hear, the guidance of our soul is an ongoing choice that may be repeatedly tested.

Sometimes we think of choice as a matter of consumer freedom, or as a philosophical issue of free will or responsibility. While choice can have those meanings, in this chapter I wish to talk about choice as the doorway to our creative power. To unleash this power, we must begin from the state of beingness.

The Order of Creation

If I asked what would make you happy, how would you answer? This type of question is often answered with a formula that follows the order of "Have→Do→Be." "If I HAVE this, I will be able to DO that, and then I will BE happy." By this point, you can probably recognize that such an order makes your happy state of being dependent on a transient circumstance (having or doing something) and so contains the seeds of its own failure.

Allow me to reverse this formula. The way to "make yourself happy" is to be happy. The formula thus goes in the direction of Be→Do→Have. We *begin* by being in whatever state we wish to attain.

Being is a more awakened state than having. To be is to exist in a space of pure choice and creation. It is a state of immense power. "I am happy. I am generous. I am…" These statements are declarations of self-evident truth. Once you decide to be, and to allow that *beingness* to permeate every cell of your body, then your brain has the potential to create every experience and manifestation related to *that state of being*.

The natural instinct of a healthy brain, moreover, is to take action. If we know we are something, then our brain will lead us to take the appropriate action→Do. If we are happy, then we will act like one who is happy. These steps create a powerful virtuous cycle. Being happy leads to happy actions, which create greater happiness.

The subsequent state of "have" is almost incidental. The awakened soul has already achieved its purpose just by beginning from its chosen state of being. Yet, beautifully, *having* is also a natural outcome of consistent habits of being and doing. A woman who is happy will laugh a lot and live with vitality. Inevitably, she will have warm relationships and bountiful opportunities that reflect her habits of happiness.

Beginning from a state of true *beingness*, then, is to succeed before finishing, and to plant the seeds of havingness which an enlightened soul does not even require.

The Gap

You might be thinking to yourself, "Well, if it was as easy as simply changing the order, then would not everyone simply do so and live happily ever after?" This is a valid question that the tools in our HT toolkit can address.

The reality is that our culture and social institutions are mostly designed around the formula of Have→Do→Be. Thus habituated, we are comfortably familiar with seeking to have. So there is a gap between our habits and our enlightened understanding. And the longer we maintain the habits, the wider the gap becomes.

Fortunately, HT provides us with tools for adjusting to our new formula of Be→Do→Have. Your soul's voice might provide some guidance. We must not stop listening to our guide. So first, let us ask our soul.

This may be challenging. We are considering something different, so we should expect to hear the loud voices of our minds and emotions, calling us back to old habits. We should be diligent in choosing to listen to our soul. If we find our bearings and reconnect with our soul's voice, the gap will steadily decrease. The energy behind our old formula will also diminish, as the energy supporting our new method grows through repeated practice. Let us now turn to several HT tools which can accelerate this process and help us bridge the gap.

Meditation: Being in the Present

Previously, I said that meditation need not mean sitting in a special posture. Nonetheless, we can use certain physical and mental exercises to calm the noises of the mind and body, and sensitize us to the sound of the soul. The key to meditation is to exist one hundred percent in the here and now. It is a constant reawakening to this moment, as a new beginning and new opportunity, shedding the past for the pure choice of the present.

You may be thinking, "I know what kind of life I wish to lead. Until now, I have lived a life that is so far from that. Do I even have the right to wish for such a life purpose? Will I be able to live as I choose?" Whenever these thoughts come up, return to the present. No matter who we were up to just a moment ago, no matter what situation we were in, nothing can detract from our new choice in this moment—now. Nothing in the past can diminish the sacredness of the present.

By awakening to the novelty of this moment, we can more easily choose our life purpose and exist according to that purpose. Our power of creation will grow and meditation is its potent fertilizer.

For your HT toolkit, I suggest a dynamic form of meditation called bow meditation. This meditation simultaneously strengthens and makes your physical body more flexible, improves your energy circulation, and reliably helps you to hear your soul's voice. The synergy of these benefits can be extraordinary.

BOW MEDITATION

Bowing is one of the most humble and spiritual acts a human can perform. It is an action that simultaneously signifies acceptance and a deep understanding of and feeling toward its object. Through bowing, we accept, understand, and feel our soul. Moreover, through this action, we cast aside the narrow confines of the self and accept the energy of the universe.

I call bow meditation "sincerity meditation," because we awaken to the nature of sincerity in the process of bowing. This meditation involves motions through which we become one with the universe. We are connected with the energy of Heaven when we spread our arms. We are connected with the energy of earth when we bend at the waist and lay our upper bodies on the floor.

Choose the number of bows you wish to perform. Bow meditation is also a good meridian exercise. During the meditation, your lower back will be strengthened and your Dahn-jon will become warm.

1. Calm your mind and put your palms together in front of your chest. Move your hands downward and outward, stretching out your arms and moving them in a large circle until your hands are together above your head. As you move your hands upward, inhale and feel the energy of the earth and imagine your hands lifting this energy upward.

2.   With your palms together, arms extended straight above your head, feel energy connecting to your Baek-hwe (crown of the head) through your fingers.

3.   Keeping your palms together, slowly lower your hands in front of your chest, connecting the energy gathered by your hands in a straight line past your Baek-hwe to your chest.

4. Still keeping your palms together, bend forward at the waist. Bend your upper body forward and downward as far as you can. The deeper you bow, the more humility will empty your mind.

5. Kneel with the tops of your feet touching the floor and sit on your heels.

6. Bending forward at the waist and neck, stretch out your arms completely so that the palms of your hands touch the floor. Turn your palms upward and lift your hands, exhaling. As you do this, lowering your upper body as far as you can, convey your gratitude to heaven and earth and feel your soul in your chest.

7. Turn your hands so that your palms face downward again and raise your upper body. Kneel and bring your palms together in front of your chest, and then stand up.

Self-Declaration: The Voice of Creation

Another HT tool that I would like to introduce is self-declaration—the voice of creation. A declaration is not an explanation or description. It is not tied to comparison or to circumstance. It is pure choice. Our declaration reflects our being, here and now. No reasons or justifications are necessary.

Since self-declaration is the voice of creation, it is one of the most powerful ways of expressing our passionate life purpose. Our declaration creates a new possibility from Nothingness (Mu). Listening to the voice of our soul as thoughts and emotions recede into the background, we journey to that place of emptiness. From there we declare ourselves to the universe.

Once you have discovered your declaration, write it down. Say it over and over. Shout it from a mountaintop or tall building. Talk to a supportive friend or a mentor about the life you envision. Declare yourself consistently, diligently, and sincerely. Your declaration is truth.

Practicing Your Declaration: Creating Character

So far I have presented life purpose as a core issue of Human Technology. I have proposed that life purpose is realized through the awakening and choice that arises from listening to your soul. I view the process of spiritual awakening and fulfilling our life purpose with passion as the core of a spiritual life.

Although we hear and feel the voice of our soul, we cannot see it. Only we know whether or not we are living for the growth of our soul. But, if there is a marker that can show this to others, it is our character. Although the soul cannot be seen, our character shows our soul's level of growth.

We make choices in the midst of a hectic world and a multitude of relationships. We act according to these choices and are evaluated on these actions. That evaluation gives us a chance for self-reflection, after which we may decide to choose anew. Through this process of choosing, acting, and reflecting, our thoughts, actions, and habits evolve. During this process we may face hardships and suffer setbacks. However, with honest and diligent deliberation, we learn to be more introspective.

In this sense, our spiritual emergence requires our full engagement with society. Our relationships and communities serve as the best environment for our spiritual development. The people we meet in any context, with whom we interact, work, and play, are all partners for our growth. Just like us, they have an inner voice. They, too, realize the transience of life. Just like us, they may be struggling with the meaning of their lives, and they are growing through their experiences. By declaring that we are partners and playing well together, we are all that much closer to realizing a community founded on enlightenment.

When Choice Dissolves, We Have Arrived

We all have something inside that is steady, even among our many emotions that come and go with our life's joys and sorrows. At the center of our consciousness, a being quietly watches us. When we are struggling in despair, that being gives us strength not to give up, and stirs our hope by saying, "It is all right."

In spite of the hope offered by that being—our soul—one nagging question might remain: "How do I know when I have found my true life purpose?"

You may recall that earlier I wrote about choice. I emphasized that we must repeatedly choose to listen to our soul, practice meditation, repeat our self-declaration frequently, and rely on our family, friends, and co-workers as partners in creating our life purpose. Each moment of every day, we make choices. Sometimes our choices are empowering, and other times they may lead to disillusionment. But we continue to choose. Even by not choosing, we have made a choice.

Through choice we see more clearly that our world is transient. With this understanding, we should not be disheartened if our life purpose evolves as well. But how will we know when we have finally arrived?

The realization of our soul's purpose will be apparent by the *dissolution* of choice. Choice disappears when we pursue our purpose with total passion. We become one with our purpose, and the possibility of moving otherwise no longer enters the mind. Our passion is reflected by the spark in our eyes and the lightness in our step, propelling us beyond any obstacle, through any hardship, until we breathe our final exhale with a smile on our face. In living out our life purpose with passion, we discover unimagined treasures.

As we progress on the soul's journey, we encounter the source of love and oneness that exists beyond separation. We come to know that this source exists inside all others as well, for their discovery. Compassion for ourselves, for others, and for the earth all flow out of such awareness. And healing begins.

My Journey with the Soul

Allow me to share my journey with the Soul.

When I was young I was haunted by endless variations of the question, "Why?" This occurred to the point that I could not focus on my studies. These questions haunted me until my late twenties. Even after I got married and had two sons, they did not go away. I lived everyday diligently, but I did not know why I was here or what I was living for.

After finishing a hard day's work, I would return home, spend time with my family, then lie down on my bed. A deep sigh would escape from me. Living without knowing why was not truly living. It got so that I could not stand to live like this any longer, and so I swore my life to a path of spiritual training and practice.

After contemplating for a long time, I went to the mountains. I vowed not to come down until I had found the answer for which I had been searching. For the next twenty-one days I did not eat or sleep, driving myself to the brink of death in my struggle to know. At the very end of my journey, a clear voice rang out loud within me: "My energy is Cosmic Energy, my mind is Cosmic Mind."

I realized that I was a flower blooming from life. I was enlightened to the truth that I was a phenomenon of life. I realized that infinite life was expressing itself through me. I sensed life's divinity breathing inside of me, and that by becoming one with that divinity, I was someone who could help create a world of blessings and creation. I felt great peace and love, and a healing mind, spring forth from my heart to the world.

But a question arose. My enlightenment felt so true and real to me, but how could I know if this was true enlightenment? Is my enlightenment real? Or is it nothing but an illusion? Who or what can prove my enlightenment?

I felt that I needed to check, verify for myself, whether my enlightenment was true or not. I believed the proof lay in whether I could communicate it to the world through practice.

I reasoned that if my enlightenment was real, I would be able to communicate the peace and love I experienced to others. If I could not do this, then the experience must only be my own mistaken thinking. Enlightenment that cannot be shared is not enlightenment. Enlightenment that cannot create is not enlightenment. This is how I set the definition and standard of enlightenment for myself. Sharing my enlightenment with as many people as possible to authenticate my own enlightenment—this is my life purpose.

In order to realize my life purpose, I have designed and promoted holistic education programs called Dahnhak and Brain Respiration for people to attain enlightenment through their bodies and brains. Realizing that individual health and peace is not possible without the health and peace of all made me dedicate my life to peace education.

When I was enlightened thirty years ago to the questions within me, I thought everything was answered. However, I soon realized that enlightenment is not the end but only the beginning. The truly important thing is not knowing but *doing*. No matter how great or magnificent our enlightenment might be, it is useless without application. People say that we are what we choose. I want to bring this truth to the next level. *We are what we do*. No action, No creation. My enlightenment has grown stronger and more powerful in the process of realizing my life purpose.

My choice to find my life purpose ended thirty years ago. At that time, I felt that I had arrived. Since then I never asked myself the question, "Who am I?" I changed my question. What do I need to do to realize my life purpose? What do I need to do to put my life purpose into practice? I ceaselessly ask and find a better way. And I ceaselessly choose.

Through reflection, awakening, and choice we are able to exist as our true selves. However, this is not the end. In order for us to realize and put into practice the life purpose we have chosen, endless choices await us. These choices are different from ones you have made so far. Now the choices you make are not about finding your path. Rather, they are choices to open the path you have found.

11

The Brain is the Key

EACH DAY, WE PROBABLY THINK AT LEAST ONCE about our health, sex, or the purpose of our life. Most of us think very little of our brains—we do not think *often* about our brains nor do we think *much* of our brains. Most of us do not really understand the true nature of our brains and thus, our true values.

So let us now talk about the master controller of Human Technology—the brain. I have said that HT is a toolkit for improving the quality of life, ending our over-dependence on experts, and helping us become self-reliant. Our brain is the way to attain these goals. There is no human activity that can happen without the brain.

Understanding and mastering the HT tools presented in this book are only possible through the brain. *Optimizing our brain function is the thread that weaves together all the tools of HT.* If we were to use our brains well, we would be more creative, productive, and peaceful in our daily lives.

Everything we do in HT is ultimately intended to help us better care for our brains and improve brain function. I believe the brain is the key to all learning and human betterment. Here are some basic facts about the evolutionary history of the brain which everyone should know.

The Evolving Brain

The brain directs the activities of all our other vital organs. It processes information to coordinate our bodily functions and activities, and their interaction with the environment. Although it weighs just three pounds, the brain commands 20 percent of our blood circulation. Scientists say that the human brain is the most complicated object in the known universe. It is our brain above all that sets us apart from all other life on this planet.

Although the brain has billions of individual neurons and many different structures, I find it helpful to think about the brain in terms of its ancient history as all life on earth is connected through the history of evolution.

The brain has three major subsystems that correspond to different evolutionary eras. These subsystems are the brainstem, limbic system, and neocortex, and they are shared by reptiles, early mammals, and later mammals, respectively.

The brainstem governs automatic processes which are necessary for the most basic life functions. It controls our heartbeat, breathing, and basic aspects of arousal and consciousness. These activities are crucial to life. If the brainstem is injured, we will die in a matter of minutes.

The limbic system is a set of structures that produces emotions. These emotional systems create the approach or withdrawal behaviors that ensure our survival. For example, mammals can be conditioned to fear a situation that has life-threatening potential. Or displays of anger can ward off competitors for a scarce resource.

The neocortex is the newest part of the brain. This part of the brain underwent an amazing, rapid expansion that differentiated us, the human species, from our predecessors.

As a whole, the neocortex has endowed us with a capacity for reasoning, planning, and creativity unprecedented in the history of life on earth. It is the neocortex which is primarily

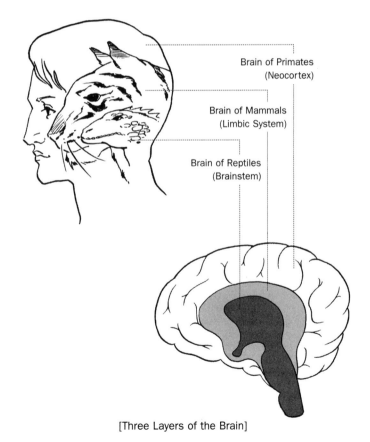

Brain of Primates
(Neocortex)

Brain of Mammals
(Limbic System)

Brain of Reptiles
(Brainstem)

[Three Layers of the Brain]

responsible for our *thinking intelligence.*

However, I contend that it is a grave mistake to think of the neocortex as the central structure of our human character. Emotions have a deep influence on our relationships, decision making, and life purpose, in both positive and negative ways. Learning to recognize and manage our emotions is a critical life task whose importance can hardly be understated.

Moreover, all my spiritual training has taught me that direct communication between the brainstem and higher structures is the ultimate source of brain power. Remember, the brainstem governs unconscious, automatic processes.

I think that in a state of high concentration, activity in the neocortex and limbic system minimizes and the brainstem is activated. In this state, you become one with your brain, and through awakening, you gain the ability to create infinitely. True creativity does not come from the knowledge stored in the neocortex. True creativity arises from the world of unconsciousness when the original life force that resides inside the brainstem, the sensibilities of the limbic system, and the neocortex are integrated as one. By learning to control this structure, you truly become the master of your life.

HT and the Brain

We vastly underestimate the power of our brains. Health, feeling and experience, physical movement, motivation and purpose—all of these are based on brain activity. The HT toolkit is designed to help you realize the power of your brain. HT stimulates your physical body; opens your energy meridians; helps you release needless preconceptions or emotional memories; and awakens you to the challenges of your life purpose. In particular, Brain Respiration (see following three chapters) is designed to help improve communication and functional integration of all your brain structures.

All life can be improved by better use of our brains. Take the best possible care of your brain. Learn whatever you can about its operation and how to keep it healthy. Learn the major acupressure points in the head and stimulate them frequently. Through better understanding and care of our brain, we gain greater confidence and capacity for mastering all our life skills.

12

BR Sensitizing and Versatilizing

I CREATED *Brain Respiration* (BR) as a program for people to gain control over their lives. Brain Respiration consists of a variety of physical, emotional, and mental exercises, progressing through five stages: Sensitizing, Versatilizing, Refreshing, Integrating, and Mastering. Each stage is directed by core principles and training methods, which I will discuss briefly in this chapter. For more details, please consult my book Brain Respiration or the website www.brainrespiration.com.

BR Sensitizing

Before we can direct our lives, we must first attain a certain level of sensitivity. Imagine being an artist who cannot tell the difference between red and blue! Our senses must be awake and discerning if we wish to make progress in any kind of endeavor.

Many teachers, myself included, have described exercises that can help you recover your sensitivity to your body, your emotions, and even the voice of your soul. Here I would like to talk about a different challenge—becoming sensitive to the brain itself! Scientists state that the brain is numb, because it has no sensory receptors. I do not dispute their laboratory findings, but allow me to offer some speculation based on personal experience.

Please notice how your brain feels when you experience different emotions or behaviors. Observing your brain takes practice and a great deal of focus, because we have to decide to do two things simultaneously—experience our emotions and notice how our brain is feeling. I believe it is possible to feel an emotion directly in the brain, before it manifests in the body.

Neuroscientists say that our personal experience of emotion is based entirely on changes in the body. An accelerated heart rate when we feel fear, or the facial muscle changes associated with a genuine smile are examples. I dispute that contention.

Try an experiment for ten days. The next time you find yourself experiencing a really distinctive emotion (joy, anger, or sadness), focus for a second on your brain. Do not be surprised if it feels, in a *physical sense*, something that very closely correlates to your emotions. Keep a record of your findings in a small notebook.

For instance, if we are experiencing joy, our brain may feel light. If we are experiencing anger, our brain may feel hot. If we are experiencing sadness, our brain may feel heavy. And you may begin to spot other bodily signals, such as heartbeat, body temperature, and perspiration, physical signals of the emotional content of your next moment. As you become comfortable with this process, you can choose to *change that moment*.

If you can learn to change a moment, you can learn to

change your life! *It is not that difficult to achieve.*

Concentrating on the brain sensations associated with certain emotions, as I am suggesting here, will soon allow us to recognize the emotionally reactive patterns that are unique to us in given situations. Then, if we become good at this, we can "head off" an upcoming emotion if it is one that we do not wish to experience!

If we can teach ourselves to "feel our brain" and watch the rest of our body for the signs that our brain is feeling a certain way, we will be able to *predict in advance* that a certain emotion is coming on. If what is emerging is an *unwanted* emotion, you can literally *tell your brain to stop doing that.*

Watching Your Body's Reactions

We are being rained upon, drenched in data, every day. Information from thousands of sources competes to get noticed by your consciousness, like children raising their hands in a classroom to get the teacher's attention.

The information that is chosen goes through a certain process before becoming reality. For many people, this process is automatic. Your brain "decides" what to look at, what to take in, and you have no conscious awareness of this process taking place.

If only you could consciously monitor this process, you would be able to gain greater control over your life. In fact, *you can.*

Through BR Sensitizing you can develop the ability to see yourself much more deeply. You begin by observing every single step of the process by which thoughts, emotions, and preconceptions are adopted and planted within your own consciousness. And you will also learn how your body reacts to certain stimuli, what emotional traps you habitually fall into, and what chains hold your consciousness in check.

This is the beginning of the healing process. Healing begins when you become aware of what you have to heal. Your transformation begins as soon as you become aware of the discomfort that your body, emotions, and consciousness experiences.

In the beginning, the transformation will consist of small things; however, as you gain experience with BR Sensitizing, you will undergo a fundamental transformation that will affect all aspects of your life.

In order to feel your brain, you need to stimulate and awaken all of your senses. Since our brain is connected to every single part of the body, feeling and exercising the many differents part of our body will also sensitize the brain. Dahn-jon breathing, meridian exercises, and Ji-gam training can be good BR Sensitizing exercises. They release tension, relax your muscles, calm your mind, and help you feel the subtle current of energy flowing through your body.

BR Sensitizing helps us become more aware of ourselves in every aspect of our daily lives. It is the first step in mastering our lives.

BR SENSITIZING EXERCISE

This BR Sensitizing exercise trains you to feel your brain through the energy in your hands. Since our hands are most sensitive to the flow of energy, even beginners can easily feel the energy between their hands. As you concentrate on your hands and massage your face and head, you will feel the vibration of energy.

What does the brain's energy vibration feel like? Although it varies from person to person, the sensation feels similar to that felt during Ji-gam exercises (see Chapter 4)—a tingling, prickling, or tickling sensation. No matter how small or subtle the feeling is, it is important to focus on it and let it expand.

1. If you are sitting in a chair, rest your hands gently on your thighs. If you are sitting on the ground in a half-lotus position, lightly rest your hands on your knees. Lift your right hand and turn your palm towards the right side of your face, about one to two inches from it.
2. Feel the sensation of the energy in your hand. Keeping your hand one to two inches from your face, sweep it down the right side of your face slowly and deliberately. Move your right hand upward from your forehead and then down along the contour of your head to the base of your head. Circle your hand around the right side of your face and feel the energy radiate out toward your hand. Once you have felt the energy, lower your hand slowly.
3. Repeat steps 2 and 3 with your left hand. When you have felt the energy from the left side of your face, slowly lower your hand.
4. Now raise both hands and feel the energy from both sides of your face and head at the same time.

5. Rub your hands briskly, until warmed, and gently massage your face, neck, and head.

BR Versatilizing

The second stage of Brain Respiration is BR Versatilizing. This is my "shorthand" for the process by which we become more flexible and versatile. By that I mean that we are willing to explore new ideas or solutions and entertain notions we have never considered before.

In today's slang I guess this is called "thinking outside the box." It is when we are versatile enough to step away from our preconceived notions about things and consider the possibility of a new notion that could change everything.

Sometimes this happens to us spontaneously. There are occasions when we suddenly see a familiar object or event in a whole new light. Or, when we ponder a particular problem for a long time, we sometimes hit upon a novel solution that surprises us with its innovation.

These occasions spring from the plasticity that is inherent to the brain's neural circuits. BR Versatilizing is intended to open our brain to new information and make it more adaptable to new experiences and situations.

The Origin of Preconception

Our preconceptions prevent us from being flexible in thought. Your preconceptions feel natural because you are so used to them. And because they are so natural, you do not even notice that they are there. Each one of us has a unique way of looking at things because we each have a particular set of preconceptions that color everything we observe. We do not even know that we have these preconceptions. And even if we do, we have a difficult time prying ourselves from the intellectual and emotional patterns that these preconceptions have imprinted upon our brain. Therefore, we have a very difficult time accepting new perspectives or opinions.

Our preconceptions were formed through our personal experiences and the socioeconomic culture in which we were raised. Therefore, it is doubly difficult for an individual to break out of a cultural preconception. Even if one were to break out of a certain cultural preconception, it is far more challenging than to actualize one's newly found conceptual liberties through actions. You would need extraordinary judgment, courage, and a sense of responsibility.

We have preconceptions about virtually everything in life, from self-identity, to gender roles, to common courtesy, to ideas about appropriateness, concepts of ownership, thoughts about money, fantasies about love, definitions of success, and much, much more.

When you "versatilize" your brain, you gain the ability to see many of these same things in different ways, enhancing your own powers of creativity. With an open and flexible brain, you will encounter even the minutest situations with a novelty and freshness that will trigger the most innovative solutions possible. Your life will become richer.

To be able to see things in different ways gives us the distance and space to become more understanding. It allows us to spend time in another person's shoes and see things as others may see them more easily, leading to better and more harmonious relationships.

The End of Resistance

If our brain resists new information or perspectives, each new piece of data will take much longer to be assimilated, triggering a series of delays that will ultimately bring the whole system crashing to a halt.

We are constantly forced to adapt to the next big thing, whether it is a new computer or a new administration. Our world is changing at an increasingly rapid pace. We have to continually learn new things and adapt ourselves to new environments and surroundings.

Being challenged by new things makes life interesting; however, such challenges are also stressful. How well we adapt to new environments depends on how flexible and versatile our brain is. When you are open and flexible, you do not have to be stubborn. Change is just a natural part of everyday life. Adapting to these new changes becomes a challenge, a joy, and a life-affirming experience.

Finally, a flexible and versatile brain will make us more capable of multi tasking. Our brain will be less resistant to processing new information, allowing us to switch back and forth between different windows of awareness as we tackle multiple tasks that simultaneously require our attention. *The importance of this skill cannot be overemphasized, given the constantly changing nature of our world.*

Moving Beyond Limitations

I encourage people of all ages, children and teens, the middle-aged and seniors alike, to move past the limitations of their mind, thoughts, bodies, and *ideas about things*, including, perhaps most important, their ideas about themselves and what they can and cannot do.

Those ideas have nothing to do with you. They are not you. They are not who you are. They are ideas, nothing more and nothing less. Remember that thoughts are inert data. They do not turn into reality until they are placed into a body. The thing to know is that you can take a thought about you that has been placed into your body and throw it out of your body. You can release it. You can let it go. You can see it for what it is: nothing but an idea. And it is not even a good idea! It is a bad idea. And you can get rid of it.

When your brain is "versalitized," so are you! When your brain is freed up to think of things it has never thought of before, you will DO things that you have never DONE before, and you will discover that you are BEING things that you have never BEEN before. You will discover that you are courageous, daring, capable, resourceful, confident, and, ultimately, the master of your life. This is the goal of *Human Technology.*

BR Versatilizing Exercise
Our brain controls every single movement that we consciously

make, from a crooked finger to the subtle curve of a smile. Each movement is connected to a specific part of our brain; working on specific parts of the body will stimulate corresponding areas of the brain.

We have an established pattern of movement and exercise in our daily lives. Even if we work out at a gym, we tend to repeat the same motions over and over again. This means that we are stimulating identical parts of the brain again and again. If we want to stimulate less frequently used areas of the brain, then we must work with parts of our body that we have neglected. We must engage in new patterns of exercise, which is what we aim to do with the BR Versatilizing Exercise below.

Try new exercises with different rhythms, especially concentrating on left and right brain coordination, to stimulate and introduce flexibility into your brain.

1. Place both hands on your chest, with one hand in a fist and the other open. With the open hand, rub your chest up and down. Simultaneously, tap on your chest with your fisted hand.
2. Repeat ten times and then switch hands.

3. Repeat ten times and switch hands again.
4. In the air, draw a circle with your left hand and draw a triangle with your right.

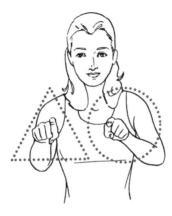

5. Next, draw a square with your left hand and draw a reverse triangle with your right.
6. Alternate hands and repeat the steps above.

13

BR Refreshing and Integration

BR Refreshing is the third step in Brain Respiration. It can be divided into two parts. In the first, we free our minds of negative preconceptions and unwanted memories. Second, we fortify ourselves against the influence of destructive information.

Our brains are constantly receiving information. According to the meaning we assign to this data, we may act in a healing and nurturing fashion, or we may act in an antagonistic and harmful manner.

Facts and Interpretations

When we allow a preconception to rule our behavior, we are actually allowing our past to control our present and future. Information that has been processed, by its very nature, is what has happened in the past. In simpler terms, the past is just another set of data. The past exists in the present only as a piece of information. We often speak of the past as if it were still alive; however, in real terms, the past has no material or physical form —it has literally passed.

We cannot change the past. We cannot change the past because it no longer exists, but traces and consequences of our actions in the past exist in the present. When we realize that the past is only information, we will have taken our first step towards freeing ourselves from it.

Information that makes up our past can be subdivided into facts and interpretations. For example, imagine that someone slapped you in the face. How long does it take to recover physically from the impact? A few minutes? A few hours? However, the insult or emotional hurt from the slap can last far longer. Therefore, what really affects us is not the physical slap, but our interpretation and analysis of the slap.

There is a story of an ancient Korean Buddhist monk that cleverly illustrates this concept. He was on his way to a distant land when he stumbled into a dark cave. Exhausted by his efforts on the journey, he chose to spend the night inside the shelter of the cave. He was fatigued and thirsty.

As he groped around, he found a small bowl filled with the coldest and most refreshing water he had ever tasted. He drank it and had a really good night's sleep. The next morning he awoke and found, to his horror, that the bowl was actually an inverted human skull inside which dew and rainwater had gathered. What had been notably refreshing the night before suddenly became nauseating. In that moment, the monk's realization of his shifted perspective triggered his enlightenment to the relative nature of fact and perception.

Our analysis and interpretation of the facts is more important than the facts themselves. Our past is a collection of our *interpretation* of what has happened—we just call it "my past" and give it a life of its own.

The past forms the foundation upon which we make today and provides a reference point for our future. However, we should not let this past gain a foothold into our present or future, especially if it contains information that we would interpret as negative.

Believing in Ourselves

In order to overcome negative information, we need most of all to believe in ourselves. However, self-affirmation—crying out, "I can do it!"—is often not enough in most cases.

Becoming truly self-confident involves an overhaul of the basic operating system that runs our brain. In order to gain that confidence, we need to prove to ourselves what type of a person we really are, or what we are capable of.

The only way to prove ourselves *to* ourselves is through our actions. Only then will we convince our brain that we mean what we say. Such self-confidence and belief will not come in an instant. We have to earn our own trust over time, by being consistent in our actions and words. This is called *integrity*.

When we have produced integrity and thus gained real self-confidence, we will not be vulnerable to the negative information that may block our path.

It is also important to protect our brain from the negative information that surrounds our consciousness daily by using the right values and principles.

A healthy life philosophy protects us from informational viruses. Values and principles can be our guiding light. They are like the white blood cells of our immune system, preventing intruders from doing harm.

BR Refreshing Exercise

As explained previously, we have a system of meridians, or pathways, along which energy travels throughout our body. Acupressure points are the points through which energy enters and exits. The top of the head is the location of the acupressure point called *Baek-hwe*, which means, directly translated, "the point of interchange of *one hundred acupressure points* of the body."

When you concentrate on the *Baek-hwe* point, along with the natural rhythm of your breathing, you can feel energy coming in through the top of your head. This exercise uses the energy coming in through the *Baek-hwe* to refresh the brain. After this exercise, you will notice that your brain feels lighter and fresher.

1. Sit in a comfortable position and place your hands on your knees, with your eyes closed. Relax your body and mind by taking several deep breaths. Feel the stream of energy move from the top of your head down to your chest, and then to your lower Dahn-jon.

2. Concentrate on your Baek-hwe by softly repeating the word, "Baek-hwe."

3. As you breathe in through your nose, imagine a stream of energy entering the top of your head, circling around it,

and cleansing your brain of stagnant or negative energy.

4. Breathe out through your mouth with a soft "Whooh" sound, as you imagine stagnant, negative energy being expelled from your body.

5. Breathe in and out slowly as you imagine fresh energy entering and stagnant energy moving out.

6. Breathe in and out three times and open your eyes.

7. Rub your hands together until warm, and gently massage your head and face.

BR Integration

Although this world presents us with a seemingly endless variety of challenges and information, our brain is more than adequately equipped for its tasks if we integrate the various parts of the brain system. The fourth step in *Brain Respiration*, *BR Integration*, allows us to do that.

I like to think of brain integration along two dimensions: the "horizontal" axis of left and right hemispheres, and the "vertical" axis of the brainstem, limbic system, and neocortex that we talked about in Chapter 11.

Most of us have heard of the functional differences between the hemispheres: left is logical, analytic, rational, linear and verbal, while the right is synthetic, intuitive, holistic, symbolic, and spontaneous.

Probably you recognize a dominance of "left" or "right" brain traits in yourself or others. But what would our personality look like if our sides were better integrated and balanced?

Better integration could lead to better problem solving. Suppose the left side is analyzing the complex features of a problem. The right side may suddenly come up with a wildly creative solution. The left argues why it will not work, then the right suggests another solution. If the two sides are communicating effectively, then the brain will eventually hit upon a creative and realistic solution. When our brain is integrated on a horizontal plane, our left and right brains are working together harmoniously to come up with the best idea or solution.

Horizontal brain integration is also about improving communication and cooperative interaction among the functionally differentiated areas of the neocortex. The outermost layer of the brain, the neocortex is divided into different lobes, which have different functions.

These lobes are called the pre-frontal lobe, frontal lobe, parietal lobe, temporal lobe, and occipital lobe, with their fundamental activities classified into separate areas.

The pre-frontal lobe is located at the center of the front of the brain, around the specific region of your forehead. It controls the highest human cognitive functions, including judgment, induction, and deduction, in addition to controlling the movements of different parts of the body during complex exercises. The frontal lobe acts as a control tower, watching over and controlling all the conscious mental and physical activities that occur. The parietal lobe, located toward the top of the brain, controls the sense of touch, pressure, temperature, and other similar sensitivities. The temporal lobe refers to the left and rightmost regions of the brain, controlling memory and hearing. The occipital lobe, located in the back of the brain, controls sight.

Improved integration between these lobes will make the brain more effective and efficient.

Incidentally, we have meridian points on our heads that are closely associated with the regional lobes described above. In-dang is associated with the prefrontal lobe; Jun-jung is associated with the frontal lobe; Baek-hwe is associated with parietal lobe; Tae-yang is associated with the temporal lobes; and Poong-ji or Ah-mun are associated with the occipital lobe. We can use these points to stimulate the different lobes of the brain indirectly, resulting in improved efficiency and functional integration. See the accompanying diagram.

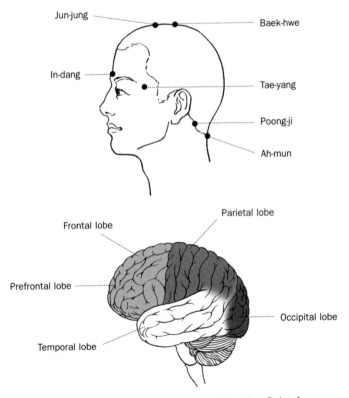

[The Brain Lobes and Related Meridian Points]

Finally, consider whether the things that we like are also the things that we consider to be right. The answer to this question speaks to whether our neocortex (thinking brain) and our lower brain (emotional brain) are interconnected. This is what I call vertical integration. We can also use the analogy of the connection between the heart and mind; if this communication is not free and natural, we will face an inner resistance to everything we do, and our actions will lack power.

A person whose sense of "rightness" coincides with his "liking" preferences is truly fortunate. The problem occurs when the two are not the same. Such a problem can bring great turmoil, as we have all experienced. Mastering our brain depends on overcoming this conflict.

I understand that, according to one view, the triumphs of modern civilization have been the consequence of rationality conquering the emotions. I suggest that rationality must be harmoniously integrated with our emotions. When heart and mind are not one, we have no passion and cannot reach our goals.

BR Integration Exercise

We have a highly developed neocortex. It is so healthy that we sometimes suppress healthy activity in the limbic system and the brainstem. The best way to tone down the activity of the neocortex and maximize the life energy of the brainstem is with a repetitive, continuous rhythm, like falling asleep to the monotonous hum of an air conditioner. Self-vibration training is a BR Integration exercise that is ideal for this purpose is. It uses repetitive rhythmic vibration to tone down the activities of the neocortex, activate the limbic system, and allow you to connect with the life energy that resides in your brainstem.

Self-vibration training is not waiting around for the body to vibrate on its own. It means that you take the initiative to ignite the vibrating reaction in your own body. There are not any set or predetermined patterns for self-vibration. You just let your body go along with the natural rhythm of life.

Release any self-consciousness that interferes with giving free rein to your movements. Do not be upset when stray thoughts and emotions enter your mind. Just let them pass.

1. Stand with your feet shoulder-width apart. Let your hands hang at your sides in total relaxation.
2. Begin by slightly shaking your knees and waist area, going up and down. Let this movement expand throughout your whole body, until every part of your body is shaking up and down in unison.
3. Gradually let the natural vibration of your body take over. Quiet your mind and follow your body as it creates its own rhythm. Feel everything in your body, including

your lips, tongue, eyes, and skin. Shake and vibrate up and down, side to side, or twisting and rolling. Your breath will naturally become synchronized with your movements.

4. Your conscious awareness will disappear as you become aware of only the vibration. Your hands will naturally go to where the blockages are, to heal those areas. Once you have passed the apex and your body feels relaxed and loose, slow your vibrating gradually and sit quietly.

5. Observe your pulse, breath, and mind. Calm your breathing and let your consciousness dwell in your lower Dahn-jon.

14

BR Mastery and More

The fifth and final step of *Brain Respiration*, is called *BR Mastery*. Let us look at how *BR Mastery* is achieved.

Step I: Be Aware that You Are the Rightful Master of Your Brain

In order to be the master of your life, you must first recognize that you are the rightful master of your brain, its owner and operator. You have redefined yourself as something more than the collection of your emotions, thoughts, preconceptions, and all the information and memories stored inside your brain. You are not your thoughts. You are not your emotions. You are not your body. You are not your mind. You are something that goes beyond all these things.

If you can locate yourself in such awareness, you will realize that your brain is a wonderful tool that helps you create the life you want. It is up to you, the user, to make the tool do whatever you want. You could make it heal people or harm people. All your thoughts, emotions, information, memories, and your physical body are just tools you can use. You dictate what choices you make, and what you create.

Just because you *declare,* "I am the master of my brain," does not mean that you *become* the master of your brain. You have to earn your brain's trust and respect. In order to earn the respect and trust of your brain, you have to consistently base all your words and actions on honesty, diligence, and responsibility. Only then, only when you demonstrate *integrity,* will your brain start listening to you and serving you.

Step II: Create a Goal

In order to become the master of your life, you have to have a definite goal. Any power you gain and any transformations you undergo are useless if you do not know how to apply that power.

Many of us are not clear about what we desire. When we fail to achieve something, perhaps the real reason is not our lack of ability, but our lack of a definite goal. If you do not really know what you want, you cannot devote yourself 100 percent to the task.

A vision is a goal that motivates us to realize the full potential of the brain. It can push us to overcome our limits and engage in fulfilling work. We can formulate a vision for our entire life, for tomorrow, or for the coming week.

How do we create a vision? Ask yourself fundamental questions. What is it you really want? What fills your heart with joy and delight? There is no one who can tell you what your vision is. Only you can decide.

If your heart tells you what you really want, then ask your brain how to go about getting it. Communicate with your brain in order to access the strength and ideas necessary to make your vision come true. Our soul uses our brain to deliver its messages to us. When in doubt, we can always ask our heart whether the message is genuine or not.

Step III: Take Action

Mastery means executing what you intend to achieve, consciously manifesting your intentions. There are many occasions when we choose to do something, yet unconsciously, we resist it. Sometimes an inner voice prophesizes failure.

"My job is not fulfilling at all. I am going to get a new job." "My job is still the most stable in the economy." "I really want to do something that fulfills me. If I do not change jobs now, I will truly regret it."

Deciding to choose what you want, unconsciously creating resistance, and trying to overcome this resistance happens simultaneously, so we often give up. Your inner resistance does not allow you to use 100 percent of your energy.

In a sense, you have to be simple-minded in order to succeed. I call such a simple and powerful mindset *Dahn-shim*. It is a mental strength that comes from deep within one's belly and never wavers.

When you know what you really want, then marshal all your honesty, diligence, and responsibility to pursue the goal until you reach it.

BR Mastery Exercise

This BR Mastery Exercise helps us supply the brain with information that is positive, refreshing, and delightful—information that will motivate the brain to its full capacity. The most important role of our brain is to help us fulfill our visions and dreams. Pursuit of a vision will awaken your brain's innate potential and will provide unending motivation worthy of your time and effort.

1. Set aside a specific time for meditation.
2. Sit comfortably and breathe in and out three times.
3. Lift your hands to chest level and begin Ji-gam training.
4. Once you feel the surrounding energy field, and quiet your thoughts and emotions, lower your hands to your knees.
5. Imagine that a stream of energy is entering your Baek-hwe (the crown of your head), and shooting out through the In-dang point between your eyebrows. Imagine that it is projecting a bright screen in front of you and that a

movie of your vision is playing on the screen.

6. Imagine yourself becoming filled with joy as you achieve your vision.
7. Keep concentrating and you might come up with ways to reach your vision.
8. Breathe in and out three times and open your eyes.
9. Record your ideas and thoughts in a diary.

The Brain and Enlightenment

Although I studied anatomy and biology as a clinical pathology major in college, it was through my personal experiences that I came to understand my brain. The greatest lesson came during my desperate search for the meaning of my life, when I engaged in a twenty-one-day sleep-deprived fast on a remote mountain in South Korea.

As you might have experienced, going without sleep is much more difficult than going without food. After three days without sleep, I started muttering to myself; after five days, I was not able to control my body or mind. In fact, I really went out of my mind. It was in that nearly delirious state, however, that I learned to peer into that "place beyond thought." I had to go to the very edge of conscious awareness. Only then can one access what has been called universal consciousness. Even a tiny bit of "self" consciousness can block a person from experiencing this realm fully.

When I couldn't stand any longer, I gave up in the most absolute and utter sense of the word. At that very moment, a voice rang out loud within me: "My body is not me but mine." Therefore, it followed that it was not me who was hurting; it was just my body that was in pain. It was so unbearable that I was about to give up my body. It was at that very moment, with a lightening realization, that I became aware that my body is not me but mine. I heard the sound of a huge explosion inside my head. Suddenly, my consciousness became very clear, and everything became clear.

Yet despite my ordeal, let me emphasize that this awareness does not require any kind of physical trauma or test. It is simply (as I found out later!) a matter of surrender, which can be achieved any number of ways. It is at the moment of absolute surrender of everyday consciousness that one encounters a world of non-consciousness that is, paradoxically, a dimension of new awareness.

It is a paradox. It involves entering a world of nonconsciousness while being more fully conscious than ever before. Enlightenment is becoming one with that consciousness. It is the ultimate human experience. In such a state you will realize who you truly are. Furthermore, I am wholly convinced that this state of enlightenment is a function of the brain. It is stunningly physical and spiritual at the same time.

Enlightenment is the experience of the *integration* of the body, mind, and soul. It is the experience of *congruence.* It is the melding of *All That Is,* manifested in your personal experience as *one integrated expression of the Essential Self.*

Not too many people will last twenty-one days without sleeping. And as I have said, it is not even necessary. Even if you did endure such an ordeal, there is no guarantee that your experience would bring you the answers you seek.

Instead, push your own consciousness to its very limit with fundamental inquiries about your own existence—*living inquiries* that are asked through your courageous movement through your own life. You have to be willing to risk your whole way of life to make such inquiries, and to *live the answers that they bring you.*

Doing Things the Easy Way

Because I knew that enlightenment lay in the brain, I made the brain the new focus of all my strategies and plans. I wanted to share what I understood about enlightenment. My plan was, first, to make people familiar and comfortable with their own brains and, second, to encourage them to begin living their lives *as if they were already enlightened.* This is the Big Secret of Enlightenment. When you live your everyday life as if you are already enlightened, you can raise yourself to a very high level of awareness.

Enlightened action can lead you to a state of enlightenment. It is not necessary to wait for enlightened awareness to fall upon you in order to take enlightened action. It can work the other way around. *The important thing is to develop a higher awareness of what constitutes enlightened action.* You do not have to learn to build a car from scratch before driving one. To be really honest with you, I went about things the hard way.

In any case, at least now I can benefit from my experience by showing people an easier way to become enlightened. I am trying to describe that in this book.

The more I consider the brain, the more excited I become. In particular, I am more than ever interested in the brain for its potential for peace. I have no doubt that when we create harmony with each other, when we help one another, our brains produce hormones of health and good feeling. Although negative habits and memories may block this function, the potential remains. We can recover that state of peace.

This book is a summary of all I have learned, and of the messages that have emerged from it. I offer them humbly to you as a gift. I hope that you find them valuable, as you continue your own personal journey.

In truth, I share these understandings not so much to help you as for you to assist me in moving further into my own self-realization. For it is my vision to do whatever I can to help make ours a better world, to assist in healing humanity. And this requires that you achieve your own self-mastery.

15

Family Matters

THE PURPOSE OF THIS BOOK HAS BEEN to provide a toolkit of skills for self-reliance. I hope I have been clear that self-reliance has nothing to do with being antisocial or egocentric. Self-reliance is about unleashing your creativity from its source in your highest self. The purpose of HT is not to make you independent of your fellow human beings. Rather, HT is designed to awaken us all to our mutual interdependence. The principles and skills of HT—using moxibustion, managing sexual energy, or realizing no-self—are all profoundly social. The point is to nourish and grow our interdependence in the most effective, healing, and enjoyable ways possible.

With whom will we learn to use and master these skills? The best place to apply HT is within the family. We spend the most time in our formative years of life with our families. HT is intended to help incubate love, wisdom, and power in the family, the most important unit of our society. Our families need our healing mind, the foundation of HT. Our deepest values and habits were formed within our families.

If we do not start with a firm footing in the family, then the information we receive from schools or specialists will ring hollow. Strong, loving family bonds nurtured from an early age create a basic sense of security, confidence, and trust in the world. Without these, the world seems frightful or dangerous, and our ability to function in society is correspondingly compromised.

HT is intended to help you, whether you are a parent, daughter, son, sister, or brother, heal and grow your family. I hope that HT will help our families regain their rightful place in our society, as training grounds for understanding and harmony.

Your Family Life—Past and Present

Is there any such thing as a family with no problems? I doubt it. Some of us have experienced deep trauma from abuse or living in a home twisted by an addiction. Others have had parents so dominated by a career or other goal that they may hardly know what it means to have a caring parent. Parental overindulgence brings its own problems if the child does not learn how to be successful in the "real world."

When we consider the perspectives of suffering, transience, and Mu-ah, the impossibility of a "family with no problems" becomes even more obvious. If the individual struggles when confronting these shattering spiritual truths, how much more difficult for an entire family to confront them!

Nowadays, most of us have had some chance to reflect on dysfunctional patterns from our family upbringing. If you are very psychologically oriented, you may know when some aspect of your behavior or life relationships represents an unnecessary extension of an old family habit.

As we gain greater perspective and clarity, how should we proceed with respect to the families who raised us? Depending on your circumstances, it may or may not be important for you to directly readdress some issues with your original nuclear family, to heal and remake some old limiting patterns. Only you can decide whether and when to return home to make things right. Ask yourself whether it will serve your highest life purpose to do so.

In any case, there is no question that you have the responsibility to make your own current family in your highest image of love and wisdom. You must consciously end any patterns of abuse, cruelty, neglect, passivity, dominance, or other dysfunction that has been passed on to you, and vow not to recreate it in your life today. Everyone's potential is limited by some kind of needless habit leftover from their family upbringing, and we are all stunted until those patterns are broken and remade.

The difficulty, as always, is the gap between knowledge and action. We may be aware that past anger towards a family member is the source of our needless anger towards the world, and we may still continue to act out that pattern, however pointless. After we have gained that understanding, the real challenge is, *how do we change ourselves?*

The HT toolkit is designed to help you bridge the gap between knowledge and action. All of the skills we have covered in the areas of health, sexuality, and life purpose, as well as the tools of Brain Respiration, are intended to help you change your life in the direction that you know you need to go.

Before Starting Your Own Family

If you are thinking of creating a family, please consider that health, sexuality, and the soul are core aspects of successful family management. Being self-reliant and learning basic principles and skills to manage these issues is a requirement for family leadership.

Fathers and mothers should be able to take care of most health concerns for themselves and their children, provide guidance on sexuality, and give them teachings that will awaken their passion and life purpose. Such competence should likewise be demonstrable by anyone who intends to lead other "families"—congregations, associations, organizations or groups of any kind whose members rely on their leader for emotional, physical, and spiritual support. Happiness that starts in the family is the path to a healthier society and the foundation of peace for humanity.

Healing and the Family

Over the years, my family members have always viewed me as a healer. I have an educational background in clinical pathology and Oriental Medicine, and I have made deep personal inquiries into a variety of healing methods. I have always had a passion for healing with others. Over the years, I think I simply took it for granted, especially as I built an organization and shared my vision of healing. Nonetheless, the lessons of healing and the family apply to me as well as anyone.

I got married in my twenties and my lovely wife and I have two sons of whom we are proud. Because my work often involved long hours and much travel, I was unable to spend the time that I would have liked raising and leading my family. Before I knew it, my sons were grown and off to school.

When my eldest boy graduated from college, his physical condition was not very good. The years of diligent study, stress, and a poor diet, all contributed to his being sick. He came to me and asked for my help, which I immediately gave.

I worked with him for several weeks, administering acupuncture and moxibustion as well as prescribing deep breathing and specific meridian exercises. In a short time his condition improved. His skin cleared, his eyes grew brighter, his energy strengthened, but most importantly, a smile returned to his face. When I saw his smile, I knew that I had my son back.

There are two reasons I shared this story with you. First, to demonstrate the importance of maintaining a strong connection with our families, even as work and other pressures try to separate us from our loved ones. Second, I wanted to illustrate the benefits of HT. Acupuncture, acupressure, and moxibustion can be helpful in enhancing our relationships, especially among family members.

What if each of us became healers for other family members? Could adding such an extraordinary dimension *improve* those relationships? Love and trust are solidified and expressed in the process of caring for one another. Healing is the deepest expression of our devotion. Words pale when compared to the communication that can arise through the power of healing. So HT can help us improve not only the health of our family members, but also the harmony in our family relationships.

Healing is one of the most intimate experiences. By holding intimate and sincere conversations about health, followed by loving treatments of acupressure and moxibustion, a basis for trusted communication and deeper personal experience of our bodies develops. Children become less self-aware and embarrassed about their physical selves, leading to greater confidence and more enjoyable experiences later in life. Parents become more open to each other because healing the body mends more than just our bodies. The heart and soul are ultimately healed by the expression of mutual trust and love.

Our Most Important Guideline

If your child asked you right now, "Mom, Dad, what do you live for?" How would you answer?

I know how challenging this might feel for you. "What would I say about the purpose of life to my children?" I believe the significance and weight that this challenge presents is an expression of how much we love them. As a parent, we wish to give them the best answer. In order for us to provide what might be the most invaluable guidance, we must first ask ourselves, "What do I pursue in my life?"

The most precious gift we can give our children is to let questions of the purpose of their existence grow naturally in them, and respond to their questions with the wisdom we have gained from our life experiences. Of course, our answer doesn't automatically become theirs. They will each find their own path in life. It may be vastly different from ours, or it could be one that is an extension of our experience. In either case, having a sincere exchange about our passion and life purpose gives our children confidence. Their trust and respect for us will grow.

The Healing Family Movement

Because the HT toolkit can be beneficial to our families as they strive to positively contribute to and build strong communities, I have tried to put the tools in their hands through the Healing Family Movement.

The Healing Family Movement, powered by HT, is dedicated to providing comprehensive resources for families to flourish, subsequently invigorating the roots of a healthier, more peaceful culture.

The Healing Family Movement supports families in maintaining or regaining their health, strengthening their familial bonds, and creating a robust, balanced life. Through a worldwide network of Dahn, Brain Respiration, and Healing Family Centers, we are creating the infrastructure for a movement to transform the globe. The *Resources* of this book outlines further HT teaching tools. Moreover, many HT professionals are being trained to further enable families to confidently regain their leadership role.

Enduring families ensure the stability and strength of society. While some alarmists claim the demise of the family, I am quite sure that the seeds of any meaningful societal change will first be sown in our homes.

16

Heightened Sense of Perception

SEVERAL YEARS AGO WHEN I WAS IN SEDONA, ARIZONA, I heard
this from a man whom I will call Mark:

*About two years ago, I had a stroke. The stroke left me with
serious speaking disabilities and my arm and part of my leg
were paralyzed. At the time I had been overwhelmed with stress
and fatigue while trying to expand my business.*

*I was fortunate enough to live through it and go through
rehabilitation to recover. Yet, my biggest problem was the fact
that I smoked. Smoking is terrible for stroke patients, but even
upon hearing from my doctor that I was never to smoke again,
I couldn't quit. I tried everything. But the thought of a cigarette
would stay in my head all day, preventing me from thinking
about anything else. I found and took part in many smoking
cessation programs, tried nicotine alternatives, and acupuncture. I tried everything, but it seemed I would not be able to quit*

smoking on my own. Even though I was still suffering from the after effects of my stroke, I couldn't stop myself from smoking a pack a day. My wife griped over the fact that I was incredibly swift and strong with business decisions but could not even quit smoking.

I started Dahnhak training when a personal trainer suggested meditation for relaxing and relieving some of the tension in my life. I went to regular classes twice a week at a Dahn Center nearby. When I was away on business trips, I did meridian exercises and abdominal breathing on my own. And I kept up with meditation practice everyday.

About four months after I started, I got up in the morning and just like any other day I went into the bathroom and lit up a cigarette. But as soon as I took a drag, I felt nauseated. Thinking it strange, I took another drag and felt so sick that I had to put out the cigarette. My body automatically rejected the cigarette.

It is hard to explain how this change happened. It feels like I suddenly have a very sensitive sensor in my body and mind. This sensor helps me make better choices every moment of my life.

Our Range of Heightened Sense of Perceptions

Although there are differences in degree, everyone at some point in their lives has a moment of awakening like Mark. An inherent sense that we have in our bodies turns on. Through these moments, we are able to have a deeper human experience and expand our understanding about the world. I call this internal sensor that Mark talked about a Heightened Sense of Perception (HSP).

Perception is the process of knowing or being aware of information through the senses. Through perceptions awareness, discrimination and integration of impressions, conditions, and relationships about objects, images, and feelings are possible. When we have HSP, we have a heightened sensitivity, alertness, and ability to perceive at an expanded level aspects of life that would otherwise not be accessible. There are many ways that we can experience HSP.

The first is the physical ability to perceive subtle changes in the body. our body has the ability to monitor its health and return it to a healthy state. This is our body's healing capacity. If our body is in need of water, we feel thirsty and look for water. If we are cold, our body shakes to produce heat. If we are hot, our body sweats to cool off. Our immune system takes care of foreign bodies that enter. Even recovering from a cold or the way our skin heals after a cut is a result of this capacity.

One of the most obvious signs that our physical sense has developed is that our body's balance and power increase. We have reserves that compensate when we are challenged by some kind of stress, and we have vitality. Our body desires that state. When our physical sense develops, our bodies know that state of balance and seek to maintain it. Mark was able to automatically quit smoking because his physical sense was activated. The meridian exercises, abdominal breathing, meditation, and moxibustion introduced in Chapters 4 and 5 are practical techniques that will strengthen this kind of physical sense.

The second way we can experience HSP is through an energy sense that allows us to perceive the flow of energy that permeates the world. Life itself is energy, and energy creates the flow of life that cannot be contained. Energy is ceaselessly in motion, coming together and spreading out and making up all life forms. You and I and all phenomena are ultimately manifestations of energy.

All life forms have the ability to feel the subtle flow of energy. However, because we have become increasingly disconnected from nature and dependent on language to communicate and our five senses for perception, our ability to distinguish energy has been diminished.

When one's energy sense is developed, one's self-healing mechanism increases noticeably, and one is able to relate to nature and other people more intensely.

The development of our energy sense is intimately connected to the development of physical sense. It is only after the physical sense is awakened to subtleties that the energy sense can be developed easily and more deeply. Ji-gam (Energy Sensitivity Training), introduced in Chapter 4, is especially effective in developing this proficiency.

The third way to experience HSP is with a spiritual sense that helps us to pursue values that are rooted in our soul. If we do not know our souls, then we are trapped in the physical body. Because the physical body is confined to space and time, it believes that it is alone, finite, and separated. But when we awaken to our soul, we feel our connection to the universe. To awaken our spiritual sense, we must listen carefully to the voice of the soul (see Chapters 8–10). We can develop our spiritual sense and strength when we choose to live as our soul's voice directs, with honesty, diligence, and responsibility.

The key to our spiritual sense lies in our experience of peace. This is when human beings experience a heightened sense of well-being and an enhanced awareness of who they really are, thereby moving to the realm of human consciousness that is otherwise inaccessible: a place of peace.

A final way to think about HSP is the ability to use our "sixth sense" to perceive objects or events without use of our five sensory organs.

Like other senses, we can train and sharpen our HSP. The energy sensitivity training exercise below demonstrates how our HSP can be awakened.

HSP Energy Sensitivity Training

1. Fill up three identical glasses with equal amounts of water, orange juice, and milk.
2. Close your eyes and place your hand with palm facing down about 2 inches above each glass to feel each liquid. If you focus on your palms, each liquid will feel different. Open your eyes to check which one you are feeling and close them again. Repeat this several times.
3. Close your eyes. Have someone change the order of the glasses.
4. Feel each one and try to identify each liquid.
5. After stating the order, open your eyes to check whether you are right.

A Compass for Navigating HT

Throughout this book I have stressed that I wish for you to regain and actualize your own creative power. You need not rely on outside authorities to manage the majority of activities related to the core issues of your life. I am quite confident that if you grasp and apply the principles and skills of HT, your life will be richer, more authentic, and more peaceful. In order to use HT wisely and effectively, however, you need good judgment.

In a sense, much of our modern world is about the replacement of individual good judgment with institution-based knowledge. In our reaction against dogmas of the pre-modern age, we have created high technology systems and the rule of specialists—all of which are characterized by standardized analysis of sensory data. The knowledge thus acquired may conform to certain standards of predictability, but I submit that it is not a basis for living a life of passion and purpose.

Again, my point is not to reject technology, systems, and specialists. I hope I have made clear that they should not rule your life.

In order for us to be the masters and not servants of technology, we must be confident in our ability to make choices that reflect our most important values. We can only make these highest choices when we are well informed and have access to all the data that pertain to our situations. If our information is restricted to the data gathered with the blunt tools of our five senses, then our life course is automatically restricted to the realm of these gross physical phenomena alone. Do we really desire such lives for ourselves and our children?

The way home to self-reliance depends on regaining confidence in our good judgment. By its very definition, good judgment is not a product of logic, analysis, or systematic thinking. Good judgment is the internal compass that guides us when such thinking is apt to confuse us.

Developing HSP is a way for you to reclaim your internal compass. HSP helps wisely guide your use of HT or any other form of technology.

HSP in Action—the Power of a Smile

I always keep a blank piece of paper on my desk in case I need to jot down ideas. I often use a traditional Asian writing brush because I find it more conducive to expressing images and ideas that are sometimes difficult to express in written words. Pens and computers are very convenient ways of conveying messages. However, I often wish to capture the moment-to-moment sensation of existence through the vibration of energy—something outside the bounds of language. For that purpose, a stroke of a twill brush, a tap on a drum, or a few notes on a flute are all effective alternatives.

When I agonize over an issue, thinking deeply, I enter a meditative state. Then, at some point, I achieve a nonconscious detachment in which I find a creative solution to a problem. That is what happened several months ago.

In a state of detachment, I felt something move within me. I dipped the brush in ink and brought it to the paper. I found myself drawing a round shape with several dots: it was the smiling face of a person. Then I found myself compelled, perhaps by the freshly drawn smiling face, to move my brush over the paper a few more times, to the left and right. I had drawn a waving hand. As I put down the brush, my face formed an expression that mirrored the smile on the paper.

After a few days, I put the picture up on the wall. As I looked at it one morning, I realized that the picture was a perfect representation of HSP phenomenon. When HSP is fully developed, a 'smile' is the expression that graces people's faces. I decided to use the picture as a symbol and call it the "HSP smile." Then another thought came to me. HSP can also stand for Health, Smile, and Peace. This HSP smile could be used as a symbol for the Healing Family Movement.

HSP guides us to health, happiness, and peace. Its arrival is marked by a smile on our faces. One smile will bring another smile, creating an unending chain that will infuse individuals with health and happiness, and our society with harmony. As I gaze at the HSP smile, I imagine your radiant face and a peaceful planet earth.

17

Creating Tomorrow Together

HUMAN TECHNOLOGY IS A TOOLKIT OF the most effective tools that I have shared for people's personal growth and social enlightenment for over twenty-five years. I offer these tools not only as self-reliance tools that can improve the quality of life, but also as educational guidelines for creating a happier and more peaceful society. I truly wish that HT will be used widely for healing individuals, families, and our communities. In closing, please allow me to share the three central values that have motivated this book and all my life work: earth, peace, and completion.

Earth

The values and beliefs we hold today are a reflection of our times. We should not make the mistake of thinking of them as eternal truths. Compared to the history of humankind, much less the age of the earth, these beliefs are less than a blink of the eye.

Earth is the most enduring thing that humans experience. No faith or beliefs of any kind are older than the earth. Placing the earth at the center of our value system is an obvious choice.

If we recalibrate our ethical and moral universe relative to the earth, then our stubborn beliefs about nations, states, and religions no longer seem so important. We realize that temporary, relative values have motivated pointless, small-minded warring throughout the millennia.

Only when we place the earth at the center of our value system and respect one another as fellow *earth humans* will we have found the basic foundation of peace.

Words can hardly do justice to the brother and sisterhood of humanity that I feel and wish to realize. Sometimes we have to invent a new term. In order to realize my soul plan I have created what I call the Earth Human Movement.

I use the words "earth human" to describe the state of consciousness that we will attain once we have experienced awakened awareness and have decided to take enlightened action. To become earth humans means that we realize and practice the oneness that connects us all.

Since the earth existed before nations, religions, or ethnicities, our self-identification with the earth takes primacy over our self-identification with any other artificial classification. When we acknowledge the earth as the center of our values, then we can recognize ourselves as earth humans, first and foremost. The fact that we are earth humans is also so obvious that it takes a while to realize. Before we are Americans, Koreans, or Japanese, we are earth humans. Before we are Muslim, Buddhist, Jewish, or Christian, we are earth humans. Earth human is, in fact, our truest identification.

If we redefine ourselves as earth humans, the chains of names, religions, ethnicities, and nationalities and their associated preconceptions will not limit us. When our highest common identification is as earth humans, then we will be fueled with courage to throw off the yokes of small-mindedness in any form. The future of our species itself is at stake.

Peace

We are all familiar with the state of peace. Peace is the natural state of mind of an earth human. Peace is not an abstract concept, a negotiated settlement, or a state of passivity. It is a state of human *beingness*. While peace partly depends on external circumstances, in our core we know that fundamentally peace begins in the individual. All HT skills are intended to develop, as a goal or side effect, our capacity to actualize peace. Peace must be felt as a bodily experience that we can consciously share with our fellow humans.

When peace has thoroughly permeated our brain, mind, and body, we can create it as our reality. I firmly believe that every person is a peacemaker, once they have developed their self-awareness and creativity. Peace must not be left to government leaders or gurus. It must spring from the brains, hands, and minds of the people.

Completion

The third central value is what I call "completion." Completion is different from perfection. Perfection, as a state that describes the absence of faults, uses comparison and evaluation as evidence of its being. Completion is a wholeness that includes both perfection and imperfection. Completion trumps competition every time and creates a game, not of winners and losers, but of winners and winners.

Success is a relative term; it is a state of being as judged by and compared to others. Success can be achieved through money and fame; however, completion can only be achieved when you know and achieve your mission in life. Competition is necessary for success, but completion does not require competition. Only the winner may drink from the cup of victory in competition; in completion, everyone has his or her own victory cup. The road to success is paved with competition; the road to completion is paved with mutual assistance.

If we accept completion as the primary purpose of life, in place of perfection or success, we have suddenly created a new context within which to decide how to manifest our highest self. Seeking to manifest ourselves as a "perfect" person will cause us to strive in one way, while seeking to manifest ourselves as a "complete" person will create entirely different behaviors.

We will no longer judge our lives by the relative measure of success in competition, but by the absolute value of completion. Completion will be the eternal goal of our newfound lives. Completion rejects nothing, least of all material success. The difference is that we manage material things towards this inclusive vision, rather than using or accumulating material objects to achieve an imaginary state of faultlessness. Living a life moving toward completion will produce the epitome of both spiritual and material success, both for the individual and humanity as a whole.

Healing

Healing is the way to realize these three values. The HT tools that I have introduced in this book are basically healing methods. This is why the Earth Human Movement was first introduced to the world through the Healing Society Movement. With the advent of HT principles and practical skills, "Healing Society" can now be more directly actualized as "Healing Family."

Recovering our desire to heal is recovering our original humanity. A society that is healthy will not rely on the letter of the law, but on the enlightened humanity of its members to grow and heal one another. The healing process begins in our homes.

If healing is a mountain, then peace is waiting at the summit —peace of the body, spirit, and humanity. It is my desire that HT empower a healing movement for the family, society, and the world, leading us at last to peace on earth and goodwill towards all.

Creating Tomorrow Together

This book does not contain the answers to all the questions you might have. The messages here are, in the nature of things, incomplete.

What I hope this book will do is convince you that there ARE answers, that life's questions do not have to be left unanswered, that life's problems do not have to remain unsolved, that life's future does not have to be unknown.

HT education is not about knowledge. It is an education that starts from a love for humanity, with the totality and creativity of the human being at its base. It is my firm belief that if families teach skills for health, sex education, and life purpose with love and wisdom, we will create a better world.

Look at this book as a family management manual. As I led this movement over the past two decades, inevitably, there were many times when I had to sacrifice time with my family. I feel deeply sorry about this. Through it all, my family has always believed in me and understood me, remaining loyal supporters. I know how invaluable family and family education are, and I feel a fathomless gratitude and love towards my own family that I cannot express in words.

The purpose of HT is the recovery of humanity, the recovery of education, the recovery of all human relationships, and the recovery of the relationship between humanity and nature. It is intended to create an Earth Human culture and the realization of peace for humankind.

The HT toolkit contains core tools, but by no means is it exhaustive. My hope is that this book provides a concise introductory map of what I have discovered while on my journey, so that your journey will be that much easier. I have aimed to summarize in one place all of my most valuable knowledge about how we can create life through our power of choice.

Take what you find here only as a beginning, then follow your own path. Individually and together, we have much to experience, much to discover, and much to create.

Let us create tomorrow together, and let us begin today.

"There is no expert for human experience.
Each of us is the specialist of our own lives.
Human Technology is about living a life of creation."

12 HT Maxims for Authentic Living

1. Return to your breath and body as tools for your health.
2. Breathe slowly, deeply and lightly, especially when you are upset.
3. Keep a fire in the belly and a cool head.
4. Celebrate your sexuality with purpose and responsibility.
5. Listen for the voice of your soul until you find your passionate life purpose.
6. Embrace suffering and emptiness as the foundation of enlightenment.
7. Live as your soul directs with honesty, integrity, and diligence.
8. Train your body so that change feels better than habit.
9. Smile and be at peace for no reason.
10. Recognize that you are what you choose and what you act.
11. When you need an answer, ask your brain.
12. Remember to exhale at the moment of death.

Resources

Where to Get Materials for Moxibustion

Moxa-rolls and other materials for moxibustion can be purchased at oriental medical clinics or Chinese herb stores. Many online sites also sell a range of products for moxibustion imported from China, Japan, and Korea. Search the internet using the key words "moxibustion supplies." You can purchase dried, packed moxa leaves and incense sticks used for moxibustion online at www.healingplaza.com.

Website for Healing Family Campaign

www.HealingFamily.org is the Healing Family Campaign's website. It is full of health tips and suggests ways to get along better with your family. The Healing Family Campaign, powered by Human Technology, is dedicated to providing comprehensive resources to help families flourish, nurturing a healthier, more peaceful culture from the ground up.

Healing Family Workshops

You can join Healing Family Workshops which Dahn Centers provide around the world. Healing Family Workshops are good opportunities for you to learn more about the principles and skills for self-reliant health care, including moxibustion. Dahn Centers also offer regular classes and special programs in which you can learn about Dahn-jon breathing, meridian exercises, meditation, and Brain Respiration. For schedules and more information, please contact the Dahn Center nearest you or visit www.HealingFamily.org. You can find the nearest Dahn Center at www.DahnYoga.com.

Books, CDs, and Videos

These books, CDs and Videos will help you become self-reliant and will teach you more about the HT health tools introduced in this book.

Brain Respiration

This book provides you with the principles and methodology of Brain Respiration, including the five steps of Brain Respiration and how to optimize your brain function.

Brain Respiration Self-Training (CD)

This CD contains precise instructions on key Brain Respiration exercises including energy sensitivity training and the five main steps of Brain Respiration.

Meridian Exercises for Self Healing 1, 2

These books include systematic series of meridian exercises that relax and rejuvenate the mind and body. The pulling and stretching motions of meridian exercises stimulate and facilitate the natural flow of energy throughout the body.

Dahn Yoga for Beginners (VHS & DVD)

This video offers an easy-to-follow, step-by-step guide to the basic Dahn Yoga (Dahnhak) workout. It includes meridian exercises to stretch the body, guided relaxation to revitalize the mind, abdominal breathing to center and quiet the mind and body, and feeling Ki energy to connect the mind and body.

Moxibustion for Common Symptoms (DVD)
This video provides you with a detailed guide to the principles of moxibustion and its application. In particular, you can learn about how to locate moxibustion points for common symptoms including headaches, stomachaches, the common cold, and the flu.

If you are not able to purchase these books, CDs, and videos at your local bookstore, you can order them online at www.bodynbrain.com, www.amazon.com, and www.healingplaza.com.

Index